Global Economic Disparity

Global Economic Disparity

*A Dynamic Force in Geoeconomic
Competition of Superpowers*

Jae Wan Chung

LEXINGTON BOOKS
Lanham • Boulder • New York • London

Published by Lexington Books
An imprint of The Rowman & Littlefield Publishing Group, Inc.
4501 Forbes Boulevard, Suite 200, Lanham, Maryland 20706
www.rowman.com

Unit A, Whitacre Mews, 26-34 Stannary Street, London SE11 4AB

British Library Cataloguing in Publication Information Available

Library of Congress Cataloging-in-Publication Data
The hardback edition of this book was previously catalogued by the Library of Congress as follows:

Chung, Jae Wan.
Global economic disparity : a dynamic force in geoeconomic competition of superpowers / Jae Wan
Chung.
pages cm
Includes bibliographical references and index.
1. Economic development--Developing countries. 2. Economic development--Developed countries.
3. International trade. 4. Foreign economic relations. 5. Geopolitics. 6. Economic history. I. Title.
HD82.C5226 2015
337--dc23
2015001565

ISBN 978-0-7391-9357-0 (cloth)
ISBN 978-1-4985-1609-9 (pbk)
ISBN 978-0-7391-9358-7 (electronic)

to ED

Contents

List of Tables

List of Figures

Abbreviations

APEC	Asia-Pacific Economic Cooperation
ASEAN	Association of South East Asian Nations
BRIC	Brazil, Russia, India, and China
CEA	Council of Economic Advisors
CPC	Caspian Pipeline Consortium
ECB	European Central Bank
EEZ	Exclusive economic zone
EMU	European Monetary Union
EU	European Union
FAO	Food and Agriculture Organization, UN
FAS	Foreign Agriculture Services
FDI	Foreign direct investment
FOMC	Federal Open Market Committee
FPI	Food Price Index
GATT	General Agreement of Tariffs and Trade
GED	Global economic disparity
GHE	Global historical event
HOS	Heckscher-Ohlin-Samuelson Theory
IEA	International Energy Agency
M&A	Mergence and Affiliations
MB	Monetary base
MNC	Multinational corporations
NAFTA	North American Free Trade Agreement
NBER	National Bureau of Economic Research
NGA	National Geospatial-Intelligence Agency
OECD	Organization of Economic Corporation and Development
OPEC	Organization of Petroleum Exporting Countries
OTCA	Omnibus Trade and Competitiveness Act of 1988

QE	Quantitative easing
R&D	Research and Development
REM	Rare earth materials
SDR	Special drawing rights
TAF	Term Action Facility
TARP	Troubled Asset Relief Program
TPP	Trans-Pacific Partnership
TSLF	Term Securities Lending Facility
WTO	World Trade Organization

Introduction

The world is a veritable stage for superpowers. There are countless historical events that occurred throughout the history. Major historical events are best viewed as the outcomes of games played by superpowers for their own economic interests. They are either the results of successful negotiations between/among countries or the cases of failures to reconcile conflicts of interest.

The objective of this book is to explore a hypothesis that can be postulated as: The primary cause of a major global historical event (GHE), political or economic, is the global economic disparity (GED) corresponding to the event. The hypothesis is comprehensive and its policy implications are powerful. In order to reduce international conflicts or tensions between superpowers, that is, global historical events (GHEs), it is logically correct to view that global economic disparities should be minimized. At present, however, there are only a limited number of superpowers. They may be referred to as *political oligopolists* who would consider GEDs as the best opportunity for their interests seeking. This book proposes that the world community should establish a global stage for fair competition among a *larger* number of superpowers or superpower blocs for economic efficiency and stability in the global markets.

Equilibrium is a central concept in economics. It is a steady state established under perfect competition. As a disequilibrium situation, a global economic disparity is a subject relevant to an economic analysis. However, GEDs and GHEs encompass a broad spectrum of the social science areas: economics, history, politics and geography. Such an interdisciplinary area is characterized as *geoeconomic s*. Economics alone is not sufficient for comprehensive analyses of causalities between GEDs and GHEs. Global issues and problems are often misunderstood as resolved politically. International relations are complex. The intersections between the political and economic domain are considerable. For example, Europe is dependent on Russian energy supplies. Given the two hypothetical military deals between Russia and France *vis- à -vis* Russia and the U.K., the U.S. policy toward any conflicts of trilateral interest among the United States, Europe, and Russia needs to take into account the two military deals between EU countries and Russia.

This book explores geoeconomic insights into the GED-GHE causalities by multidisciplinary inferences. In general, historical events that occurred much further down the timeline are meaningful to the current generation. This study focuses on the causal relationships between primary GEDs and GHEs that stand out since the first industrial revolution. The causation can be unidirectional from GEDs to GHEs or bidirectional between them. It confirms the causality relations on the postulated hypothesis. The recent emergence of the Asian economy is significant as an additional superpower to the global economy and should be positively regarded as the third economic bloc or the third axis that supports the global economy. Hopefully, resource-abundant Latin America or South America will emerge as a fourth major economic bloc, as the fourth axis in the future. The global economy should be more stable and prosperous with third and fourth superpower blocs. Their collaborative efforts should also be an effective way to ameliorate poverty in the third world.

This book is being written shortly after the world economy was trapped within downward spirals caused by the U.S. financial crisis in 2008 and by tensions between Europe -United States and Russia in connection with Ukraine in November 2014. In addition to pivotal countries such as the United States and euro-zone countries, Japan was already experiencing an economic slump from the impact of the earthquake and nuclear power plant disaster in 2011. Rapidly growing countries such as Brazil, Russia, India, and China (BRIC) and emerging countries in Asia served to balance out the world economy to some extent. At present, the United States and Europe are major debtors, and the emerging countries in Asia are major claimants despite adverse impacts from the global financial turbulence. However, the origin of the current crisis does not lie simply within the boundary of the financial sector or stock markets in the United States and euro countries but derives from the structural disequilibria throughout the world. Overall, it is notable that the global economy is now making hemispheric adjustments between East and West. It is mutually beneficial for all countries if the world economy becomes competitive as a result of the emergence of the Asian economies rather than the East remaining a reclusive hemisphere. It is hoped that the Latin American economy emerges and contributes to the global economy in a multipolar setting of the system.

Three parts, broken down into ten chapters, constitute this book. It proceeds from overviews and details. Different subject areas in detail are subject to the same hypothesis maintained throughout the book. Part I is an overview. It is concerned with the underlying rationales for the relationships between GEDs and GHEs. There are two chapters in this part. Chapter 1 focuses on GEDs and GHEs and establishes the causal relationships between GEDs and GHEs. Chapter 2 takes actual GEDs to confirm them as the primary causes of GHEs in the manner of one-to-one correspondence. This chapter discusses the economic emergence of China in detail. The emergence of China signifies itself as a paradigm shift of the global economy.

Part II justifies the rationale addressed in part I in the theoretical context. There are three chapters in this part. Chapter 3 deals with the open economy macroeconomic principles on international imbalances. It explains formally imbalances in the international trade and finance sectors among countries, either claims or liabilities. They are the results obtained from the balance of payments, a collective representation of international transactions in all sectors under consideration in this book. Chapter 4 discusses the financial crisis in the United States and the Fed's responses by means of a series of quantitative easing (QE) measures implemented for the period of November 25, 2008 to October 29, 2014. The QE policy is merely an example here but is important to address as a significant event in the history of the financial crisis, the central part of the global economic disparity. Chapter 5 is concerned with the impact of the financial crisis in the United States on European and Asian economies. These two chapters examine how a chronic imbalance in a superpower country (United States) eventually results in a global financial crises and continental contagions (especially with euro countries). The U.S financial crisis in 2008 was not the first serious one in the history of the financial crises in the world. However, it was unique in terms of causes and policy responses.

Part III draws parallels in the behaviors of superpowers throughout relatively recent history and looks into five area-specific GEDs and GHEs in detail. They are distributed through chapters 6 to 10. They are human capital and technology in chapter 6; raw materials in chapter 7; energy in chapter 8; environment, global warming, and water resources in chapter 9; and food, population, and poverty in chapter 10. Throughout the book, cases related to the United States and Europe, the two existing superpowers, are frequently cited for illustrative purposes.

It is natural to have perspectives on global issues illustrated by the standard theory of international trade. However, this book should not be construed as another study in the area of international trade. It focuses on geoeconomic competition among superpowers in the international markets. Competition here comprises not only economic competition but also competitions in social and political areas. Superpowers in each region or continent should preferably emerge in as a multipolar system, as suggested in the theory of customs union in international economics. But arguments addressed in this book are upheld even without a formation of such an economic integration. Given the geoeconomic subject characterized as interdisciplinary, it is not appropriate to attempt a deductive reasoning on statistical inferences customarily obtained by means of econometric techniques applied to any kind of quantum indexes. This book deals with a comprehensive subject. However, the analytical approach is consistently based on economic principles and is often confirmed by basic laws in natural sciences. This study requires massive data and information consistently from reliable sources. Data sources are the U.S. government, the IMF, the World Bank and the OECD. Among them,

Statistical Abstract of the United States published by the U.S. Census Bureau is the primary source.

So far, no research has been done on *geoeconomic* insights into the global economy that focuses on the behavior of *superpow ers*. This book is not quantitative or technical. Although the foundation of analysis is economic theories throughout the book, any level of students, undergraduate and graduate, in the areas of economics, political science, public administration, and international affairs and relations can access it. Professionals in these areas and nonprofessionals would find this pioneering work interesting for their future research. It is hoped that this book will facilitate readers' understanding of the real world.

In pursuit of geoeconomic insights into often sensitive issues and problems involving GEDs and GHEs, it is important to clarify that the author is not drawing upon any classified documents and confidential data unless they are published or officially released for public access. Excluded from this book are issues related to national security, the military, intelligence, arms races, nuclear weapons, illegal immigration, illegal drug markets, political convictions, and religious conflicts.

I am grateful to my colleagues at George Mason University for their constant support and encouragement. This book is not a collective treatise of my work done in the past, although the two are not mutually exclusive. I would like to gratefully acknowledge receipt of valuable comments and help on the earlier work related to this book, again, from Professors James T. Bennet, Donald J Boudreaux, Roger D. Congleton, Carols D. Ramirez, Willem Thorbecke, and Philip R. Wiest. Also, I would like to extend my special thanks to Professor Ingo Walter for his advice and encouragement for many years. Dr. Gary W. Davis read the entire manuscript of this book and gave me valuable comments extensively. Dr. Anthony de Carvalho e-mailed me from Europe with positive feedback on my work. I am deeply grateful to Mr. Joseph Parry, acquisition editor of Lexington Books, for his interest in my work and favorable consideration of this project. Finally, I wish to thank Ms. Sarah Craig, assistant editor at Lexington, for her impeccable editorial advice, valuable suggestions, and support. I am also grateful to Mr. Ethan Feinstein, assistant editor, production, Rowman and Littlefield Publishing Group, for his extensive queries in the process of page proofs of the manuscript. They were greatly helpful for clarifications and corrections.

Timely information and data available in daily newspapers, weekly/monthly magazines, and Internet news were essential to update the research in progress. Caroline Chung has constantly drawn my attention to current trends, along with valuable comments and suggestions for the entire manuscript throughout the period. Finally, I thank SJ for her forbearance and help preparing tables, figures, and indexes.

JWC, Fairfax, Virginia

I

Global Economic Disparities and Global Historical Events

ONE

Global Economic Disparities and Historical Events

Equilibrium is a central concept in economics. It is a state of balance between opposing forces in the market, such as supply and demand. Conversely, disequilibrium is a state of imbalance. If the market is perfectly competitive, a disequilibrium situation gravitates to an equilibrium point through the process of price dynamics. The *Walrasian equilibrium* is the stationary state of equilibrium in the absence of any external disturbances. The pattern of excess demand or supply and its adjustment path to the equilibrium point characterize the nature of the corresponding market and provide the theoretical basis for policy. The adjustment process in a competitive market is largely instantaneous.[1] Disequilibrium in the national or international market is adjusted through changes in prices in the real sector (e.g., goods and productive inputs) and the financial sector (e.g., interest rates, foreign exchange rates, and bond yields and stock prices).

In the real world, however, there are always external shocks that constantly disturb equilibria in markets. They are generated from the private or public sector, could be random or specific, and are manmade or created naturally. In addition, substantial parts of both domestic and the world markets are not perfectly competitive, as indicated by multinational and regional trade agreements that prohibit dumping and subsidy. In spite of the well-known law of comparative advantage for inter-industry trade under the assumption of perfect competition, intra-industry trade by imperfectly competitive or oligopolistic firms in big countries is significant in the world market.[2] The price mechanism under imperfect competition or oligopoly is limited, and the speed of adjustment to equilibrium in the market is sluggish. Interest-seeking behavior takes place in the

1

disequilibrium circumstances. Economic efficiency loss becomes a serious problem.

A disequilibrium should not necessarily be construed as socially undesirable. It is an important source of impetus for firms to compete in the international market and to motivate the global economy toward healthy development. The rationale here is simply the basic economic principle of dynamic process for (slow) adjustments. The driving force for this process is proportional to the magnitude of disequilibrium. *Disequilibrium is where power is generated.* The greater the disequilibrium, the faster the speed of adjustment. Disequilibrium is recurrent and the dynamic adjustment is perpetuated. Such a process is similar to the physical laws of power, energy, or gravity generated proportionally from the mass. Significant or insignificant and unequivocally identifiable or tacitly undergone, economic disparities are exposed to interest-seeking entities, are eventually magnified to conflicts of interest among countries, and often develop into major historical events as consequences of economic and political disequilibria. It is important to clarify that economic and political disequilibria in the geographical and historical contexts are referred to as *global economic disparities.*

This chapter discusses causal relationships between global economic disparities (GEDs) and historical events (GHEs), the postulated hypothesis in this book. In pursuit of economic or political interests, GEDs catalyze conflicts of interest between/among large countries. It is an interdisciplinary subject, characterized as *geoeconomics.*[3] From the geoeconomic perspective, a global disequilibrium may generate a global historical event (GHE) in the event of conflicts of interest among a few or several superpowers. The main part of world economic disequilibrium is trade imbalance. However, the world economy encompasses traded and nontraded goods/inputs and services in trading and nontrading countries. In addition to a focus on trade imbalances, it is reasonable to broaden the spectrum of world economic disequilibrium to economic disparities. The first section conceptualizes the GED. The prime cause of economic disparity between any two countries is comparative advantage (surplus) or comparative disadvantage (deficit) in the Ricardian context or different factor-intensities and factor-endowments in the Heckscher-Ohlin-Samuelson (HOS) perspective. Endowments of resources under consideration include human resources, energy, natural resources, and related areas such as environmental quality. The second section summarizes major historical events selected from relatively recent periods and explores causal relationships between GEDs and GHEs. The causalities imply that the world is, in principle, economically stable (or peaceful in a political sense without historical events) only in the absence of GEDs. The third section discusses geoeconomic perspectives on the world economy. The fourth section presents policy implications associated with the postulated hypothesis on GEDs-GHEs.

1.1 THE SCOPE OF GLOBAL ECONOMIC DISPARITY

In *Economic Report of the President* (2013, p. 213), the Council of Economic Advisors (CEA) recognizes the importance of global rebalancing. The CEA suggests that global rebalancing has been one of the Administration's major international economic policy goals for the past four years. In June 2012, G-20 nations reiterated their support for this goal, calling upon countries with current account deficits to boost national saving, consistent with evolving economic conditions, and for countries with large current account surpluses to strengthen domestic demand and move toward greater exchange rate flexibility.

The rationale here is primarily concerned with global adjustments of trade imbalances in the current account of goods and services in the balance of payments. In open-economy macroeconomics, there is a fundamental macroeconomic identity that helps to understand the CEA's statement. It is important to keep in mind that the net investment in the private sector and net spending in the public sector add up to the trade imbalance—the net trade surplus or deficit in the foreign sector. This identity provides us with a few other related implications:

- Trade deficits and fiscal deficits in a given country are positively related to each other.
- Trade surplus of a country equals trade deficits of another country.

Initially, trade deficits in a country may be viewed as solely a domestic issue of the deficit country. As the amount of imbalances accumulates over time, however, it becomes a serious problem to both countries, the country in deficit and the country in surplus. As exemplified by the Smithsonian Agreement in 1981 and the Omnibus Trade and Competitiveness Act in 1988 (OTCA), global rebalancing has been attempted through realignments of foreign exchange rates and enactment of trade laws. Global factor markets are not independent of the global commodity market. Adjustments in the commodity market and the factor market are followed often by financial arrangements as a temporary buffer.[4] A trade deficit means borrowing from abroad. In the absence of timely adjustments of a massive amount of deficits accumulated over time, the debt may lead to a financial crisis, like those in the United States in 2008 and Europe at present.

The amount of capital movements between any two countries, as reflected by their balance of payments, includes not only the total value of foreign investments but also the valuation of assets and liabilities, such as changes in the prices of securities, defaults and expropriations. The cumulated amount of deficits over time, the U.S. external debt for example, increased to the extent that the United States has become the largest debtor in the world as a serious global economic disparity. Massive trade deficits, along with the mounting fiscal deficits since 1983, required Federal Reserve to employ a tight money policy. Interest rates increased and private investment decreased. The housing market slowed down. The demand for housing decreased sharply, followed by foreclosures and Fed's quantitative easing (QE). The subprime mortgage practices and free-wheeling loans occurred at the time of the Lehman Brothers sparked a financial crisis as a result of massive bankruptcies and threatened in the United States. Amid radical fluctuations in the stock markets, the U.S. economy fell into deep and long stagnation, followed by a downgrade of the U.S. credit rating, leading to high interest rates for U.S. borrowing by means of U.S. Treasury bills and bonds. Given the close linkages between financial markets in the U.S. and EU, the contagion effect of the financial crisis in the United States directly affected euro currency markets.

In the absence of significant improvement elsewhere in the world, the United States recently came close to defaults in early October 2013 during a government shutdown (October 1-16, 2013). Imagine the doomsday of the world's biggest economy! Irrespective of other countries, U.S. debt transactions stemming from the trade and fiscal deficits have become most serious global financial problem. A mounting debt in a deficit country is comparable to the geological phenomenon of a tectonic fault where stored magma can propagate fractures along fault lines that ultimately lead to seismic waves or volcanic eruptions.[5]

The current account balance, deficit or surplus, is the main component of the GED. However, it is not comprehensive enough to cover economic disparities in all economic sectors and areas on the global scale. The GED comprises not only traded items in the balance of payments but also nontraded goods and services. It includes all finished goods, traded as well as nontraded, and all productive factors used and endowed in all countries. A disparity in oil reserves is a good example. The GED is a generalized state of disequilibrium in the world.

Table 1.1 shows per capita gross national income and gross domestic product by country and region. As of 2013, there are 196 countries in the world. A group of affluent countries like

the G-20 is approximately 10 percent of the total number of countries, implying that the rest of the world is relatively poor. There are 34 OECD developed member countries; thus non-members are relatively underdeveloped. Inter-country comparisons of per capita GDP measure GEDs without quantification in statistical inferences or an index to measure relative economic disparities.[6,7]

Table 1.1. GNP Per Capita: Selected Countries (in U.S. dollars at current prices)

		1990	2000	2009	2010[a]
1	North America				
	U.S.	23,440	34,890	46,360	46,588
	Canada	19,840	22,130	41,980	
2	EU				
	France	19,660	24,450	42,620	
	Germany	20,290	25,510	42,450	
	U.K.	16,190	25,910	41,370	
	Italy	17,420	20,890	35,110	
	EU27				31,784
3	Asia				
	Japan	27,100	34,620	38,080	33,785[b]
	Korea, S.	5,740	9,910	19,830	33,971
	OECD				
4	Africa				
	South Africa	2,890	3,050	5,760	
	Egypt	810	1,390	2,070	
	Congo			160[c]	
5	Other Countries				
	Brazil	2,780	3,870	8,070	11,239
	China	320	930	3,650	7,519
	India	390	1,406	1,220	3,339
	Russia	NA	1,710	9,340	19,833

Source: U.S. Census Bureau, *Statistical Abstract of the United States*: 2012, p. 846, and OECD,
　　OECD Factbook 2013 Economic, Environmental and Social Statistics, p. 35.
　　[a] GDP per Capita for 2010.

^b Per capita incomes for 2000–2009 are not significantly different from per capital income in 2010. It was the period of long-term economic stagnation for approximately 10 years, referred to as "the lost 10 years" in Japan. This period is followed by the earthquake and tsunami in 2011.

^c Congo is the country of the lowest per capita GNP in the world as of 2009.

1.2 CAUSAL RELATIONSHIPS BETWEEN GEDS AND GHES

Countless events have occurred throughout the world's history. History reveals that most such historical events have occurred when significant economic disparities prevail between or among large countries. This causality implies global stability in the absence of global economic disparities. It can be unidirectional or bidirectional and bilateral or multilateral. A particular case of causality is easily verifiable as universal and invariant from the correlation between a GED and a GHE confirmed at each point in time and also dictated by economic principles and natural laws.

This section investigates the causalities between GEDs and major GHEs since the European "Age of Discovery." The history of Asian exposures to the rest of world is relatively short. Since research in pursuit of global issues and problems in the absence of the Asian economy is asymmetrical, it is reasonable to focus mainly on events occurring recently. The main historical events are listed in table 1.2.[8] Each of them is summarized below. It is important to always ascertain the economic implications associated with events in a one-to-one correspondence.

Before turning our attention to establishing the correlations between GEDs and GHEs listed in this table, this section examines a number of facts, selected randomly from recent history, that illustrate the importance of GEDs as the key factor in the postulated hypothesis maintained throughout this book:

- A dynamic West and static Asia, until the mid-twentieth century and especially since the European age, followed by the American age, resulted in an affluent West and indigent East.[9] There would not be an argument between the two hemispheres without the differences in standard of living. For example, issues about and problems with U.S. Treasury bonds and dollar reserves held by China today and the emergence of China as a superpower substantiate continental disparity or the disequilibrium. (Chapter 2)
- As U.S trade deficits grew in the 1970's, the United States wanted to realign the dollar, especially with respect to the Japanese yen. The Smithsonian Agreement in December 1971 converted the fixed exchange rate system, which was based on the gold standard system

Table 1.2. Main Historical Global Events

1.	Geographical Explorations (1254–1506)
2.	Industrial Revolution (1760–1914)
3.	Discovery of New World
4.	French Revolution (1789–1799)
5.	European Expansions and Imperialism (1819–1914)
6.	World War I (1914–1918)
7.	The Great Depression (1930–1939)
8.	World War II (1939–1945)
9.	The Post-World War II Events (1946–)
10.	Oil Crisis in the 1970s
11.	Financial Crises in the U.S. and Euro Countries (2009–)
12.	Emergence of China (2004–)

Note: There are many other events written in the history of the world that are related to the subjects to discuss in this book, including events in the periods of Modern Japan (1864–1941), European Powers (1878–1914), Russian Revolution (1905–1925), Chinese Revolution (1911–1949), and wars in Korea and Vietnam during the Cold War period since 1947, and the unification of Germany (October 3, 1990) after forty-five years of the Cold War. They are not discussed in this book.

(pegged to 35 dollars=1 ounce of gold) determined at the Bretton Woods Conference in 1944, to a managed floating system. (Chapters 4 and 5)
- In response to chronic trade deficits, accumulated to billions of dollars, from two digits to three digits, the Omnibus Trade and Competitiveness Act (OTCA) was enacted in 1988. This law, the most comprehensive trade law in U.S. trade policy history, is the legislative basis for enforcing U.S. policy for fair trade.[10] In the absence of massive trade deficits, the OTCA would not exist today. (Chapter 4)
- In the absence of covered interest differentials (= interest differential + foreign exchange premium or discount) or risk-covered asset pricing in global markets, there would be no theoretical basis for arbitrage and speculation behavior in foreign exchange and asset markets. Without international capital flows by big banks and financial firms, there would not be major financial crises and their contagions. (Chapter 4)
- Low wages in underdeveloped countries are the primary incentive for foreign direct investment (FDI) and technology transfers by

multinational corporations. Without investment and technology transfers, there would be no rapidly growing and emerging countries in Asia. China would still remain in the category of third-world countries. (Chapter 6)

- The oil crises in the 1970s were the results of market failure attributed to economic disparities between oil-producing (the OPEC) and oil-consuming nations. The disparities are basically due to price differentials. If the price asked by oil-producing countries and the price paid by oil-consuming nations were the same, there would not be an oil crisis. The same rationale is applicable to raw materials across the world. (Chapters 7 and 8)
- The EU is in favor of environmental control, whereas underdeveloped countries and countries with high rates of unemployment are mostly against it. There would not be environmental quality issues among countries if all countries were equally developed or underdeveloped. (Chapter 9)
- Poverty, inequality, and social justice are largely integral issues stemming primarily from shortages of food. Disparities in food markets between poor and rich countries would not prevail with sufficient production and efficient allocation of food. (Chapter 10)

It is a matter of fact that the history of the world is written by superpowers. The GEDs, GHEs, and their relationships as discussed in this chapter presuppose the influence of superpowers. It is also important to keep in mind that each historical event is not independent of national economic interests. Every historical event has economic connections.

1. European Explorations (1200s–1600s)

The explorations of Marco Polo to China (thirteenth century), Christopher Columbus to the New World (fifteenth century) and Vasco Da Gama to India (fifteenth–sixteenth centuries) paved the way for Britain and other Western European countries, including Spain, Portugal, France, and the Netherlands, to reach out to China, India, Indonesia, America, and some African countries for exploration and their overseas markets. In those time periods, Europe was heavily influenced by mercantilism (sixteenth–mid-eighteenth centuries), the doctrine devoted to exporting more and importing less by means of protective trade policies. Many European countries obtained cheap raw materials from their colonies.

2. Industrial Revolutions (1760–1914)

The first industrial revolution, from water power to steam power in England (1760–mid-nineteenth century), was followed by the second revolution in France, Italy, Russia, and Germany (the last quarter of the nineteenth century–1914).[11] The industrial revolution as a whole increased production in European countries, required them to expand markets for finished goods and to secure raw materials in foreign countries, and generated significant economic disparities between the East and the West. The disparities intensified the economic interests of European countries in the East.

3. Discovery of a New Continent (Early Seventeenth–Early Nineteenth Centuries)

Roughly 150 years after Columbus discovered the New World, America, Europeans began to migrate to North America in pursuit of individual freedom and equality within the *laissez faire* spirit of capitalism. The civil class in the British colonies in America began to intensify demands for political participation on the basis of an economic power greatly strengthened since their arrival in America. Protests, such as the Boston Tea Party, against heavy taxes imposed on paper, glass, and tea by England and against the Sugar Act and the Stamp Act led to resistance by the thirteen colonies and then to open warfare and the Declaration of Independence in 1776. France and the new United States compelled Britain to recognize American independence in the Treaty of Versailles in 1783.[12]

4. French Revolution (1789–1799)

Amid rapid political changes in Europe during the industrial revolution, the French Revolution broke out. It was a violent political and social upheaval for freedom, equality, and brotherhood. The primary cause of the revolution was economic problems such as heavy taxes and feudal rents imposed on farmers, inflation and animosity toward the upper-class aristocrats and clergymen by urban workers, and the fiscal burden due to frequent wars. The revolution restructured social and political systems in France and the rest of Europe and provided European countries with a new momentum to create the economic foundation of capitalism. The French Revolution was influenced by the philosophies of John Locke (1632–1704), Francois Quesnay (1694–1774), Jean-Jacques Rousseau (1712–1778), and Adam Smith (1723–1790). Locke believed in the importance of knowledge based on experience and perception. Quesnay argued that agriculture is the only source of wealth. Rousseau advocated democratic government and social empowerment (e.g., the general will), and Smith suggested free markets. Both Quesnay and Smith rejected mercantilism.

5. European Expansions and Imperialism (Seventeenth Century–Nineteenth Century)

Geographical explorations helped European countries to reach out to foreign markets. The industrial revolution accelerated the European expansions. The French Revolution externalized internal class complaints of Europeans. Competition prevailed among European countries for securing colonies almost everywhere in the world. Africa was colonized by Britain, France, Germany, Italy, Spain, and Portugal; China by Britain and Portugal; India and North America by Britain; and Indonesia by the Netherlands. Large-scale waves of immigrations were launched from European countries to North America, Australia, and New Zealand. The fervor to explore and exploit new opportunities in colonies was exceedingly high.

6. World War I (1914–1918)

World War I was sparked by the assassination of the Austrian archduke by Bosnian terrorists, due to the racial tensions in imperial Austria-Hungary. It was a period of ideological collision between liberals and conservatives, conflicts of interest between factory workers and supporters of monarchy, and arguments about free verrsus restrictive trade. Nationalism, individual rights, economic rivalries among European countries, and the irrationalism of Social Darwinism emerged amid uncertainty all surfaced. In addition, there were political/military conflicts of interests in the Balkan peninsula between Germany and England, France and Russia. It was also a period of technological innovations in Germany that resulted in rapid economic growth after long stagnation. The emergence of Germany with strong naval power threatened England, France, and Russia, especially regarding Germany's interests in the Balkans. They formed inter-country strategic alliances. The German strategy was to isolate France and block Russian advancement to the Mediterranean Sea. Europe thus gravitated toward World War I.

7. The Great Depression in 1930

The Great Depression was the worst economic contraction in U.S. history. The Dow Jones Industrial Average dropped from 381 in 1929 to 230 in 1935, the real GNP decreased in 1933 by 30 percent compared to that of 1929, and the rate of unemployment increased from 3 percent in 1929 to 25 percent in 1933. Its impact on the world economy was enormous. There have been many speculations about the causes of the Great Depression, especially the highly protective Smoot-Hawley Tariff Act of 1930 and the tight monetary policy of the Fed.[13] Unlike England, which flexibly devalued its currency in response to the demise of the gold standard system (1880–1914), Germany and France maintained exchange rates and failed to absorb shocks from the deceased gold standard. This effect contributed to the rise of the Third Reich in Germany.

8. World War II (1939–1945)

This was a time period when the Great Depression seriously affected the German economy. Germany annexed Austria and the Sudetenland and invaded countries in Europe, including Poland, Norway, Denmark, Belgium, the Netherlands, and France. England and France declared war in 1939. Germany attacked Russia in the face of need for grain in the Ukraine and oil in Caucasus. For the same reason, Germany also invaded Africa to reach the Middle East *via* the Suez Canal. These attacks dragged out the war and widened the frontier beyond German capacity. The United States declared the war in 1941; the German front in Africa capitulated in 1943; Russia reached East Prussia on January 1945; and the Allies (the United States, Britain, and Canada) assaulted the Normandy coastline on June 6, 1944, soon liberating France. Germany surrendered on May 7, 1945, a week after the suicide of Hitler. German interests in a larger share of land and international markets during depressive economic situations in Europe resulted in political disasters for Germany.

9. Post–World War II (1946–)

After World War II, the world was largely divided into communist and non-communist blocs. The hostile relationships between countries in the two opposing blocs, known as the "Cold War" prevailed in the delicate diplomacies among countries. It was a period of political turmoil in many countries and military conflicts in Korea, Vietnam, Iraq, and Afghanistan. Despite tough times during recessions under oil and financial crises, international organizations such as the UN, IMF, World Bank, and GATT/WTO contributed to overall global economic prosperity and stability. The emergence of rapidly growing countries in Asia and South America brought about an optimistic future for the world economy. German unification (October 30, 1990), followed by Ronald Reagan's appeal and Mikhail Gorbachev's response on glasnost, is a political miracle and symbolizes political optimism in the future.

10. Oil Crises in the 1970s

There were two major oil crises, the first in 1973 and the second in 1978. They were due to market failure in the global oil market. Prior to the crises, the price asked by oil-producing countries and the price paid by oil-consuming countries were very different. The impact of the oil crisis in 1973 was especially large and drove the entire world into an economic downturn. A major recession of the U.S. economy, the biggest economy in the world and the biggest oil consuming nation, began with the first oil crisis. The Arab world emerged as an economic power.

11. Financial Crises in the United States and Euro Currency Countries

An enormous amount of U.S. debt resulted in a financial crisis in the United States in the fall of 2008 producing a contagion effect in the euro countries and sluggish economies in emerging Asia, including China. A long stagnation and political "fiscal cliff" crisis in the United States (after a brief period of recession along with the massive amount of debt of the biggest economy in the world, attributable to its fiscal deficits and trade deficits accumulated over time) impacted the global economy significantly. The debt led to the crisis in the following order: First, the U.S. Treasury continued to issue securities to borrow money from foreign countries. Second, the borrowing cost to the United States (i.e., Treasury bill rates) increased amid uncertainty about the economies of the United States and world in the near future. Third, due to a high degree of uncertainty and severe disparity, speculative activities became intense. Investors diversified their assets in order to minimize risk, stimulating international capital flows. Meanwhile, the U.S. dollar depreciated due to quantitative easing (QE) by the Federal Reserve. Short-term capital markets (i.e., short-term bond and stock markets) began to fluctuate radically in bubble fashion, followed by contagion of the crisis in the United States to euro countries and vibrations induced in Asian economies. The global economy was dragged into a downward, turbulent tailspin.

12. Emergence of China as a New Superpower

The economic situation of China in the world at present is entirely different from what it was during the nineteenth–twentieth centuries. Although per capita income is still very low, China's economy has grown rapidly, at an annual rate of 8–12 percent, since the beginning of this century. Taking over from Japan, China is now the second largest economy in the world, next to the U.S. economy, and is politically and economically an emerging superpower. There is a primary concern about enormous amounts of foreign exchange reserves and U.S. Treasury bonds held by China that may now destabilize the global financial market. The next chapter discusses the significance of China's status as a superpower in detail.

1.3 GEOECONOMIC INSIGHTS INTO THE GLOBAL ECONOMY

Economic research is subject to dual facets: a positive aspect (theory about what is) and a normative aspect (policy about what should be). The former pertains to the scientific domain of universally accepted economic laws and principles. It provides a firm basis for deductive reasoning on observed phenomena in economics. The latter is concerned with policy. Policy makers who pursue objective policies rely on empirical results provided by statistical inferences obtained from research. However, the geoeconomic domain lies beyond the boundary of deductive reasoning. It encompasses a broad spectrum of intra- and inter-country phenomena in almost all social science areas. No single time period in world history has been free of global events, economic and political, that virtually constitute the history of the world throughout in different geographical areas. Global economic disparities, where conflicts of interest among countries prevail, cause GHEs if GEDs accumulate over time, as exemplified by the oil crises of the 1970s and the world financial crises today. Global economic crisis requires interventions by superpower authorities including central banks and international organizations, such as the IMF for global financial stability, the World Bank for economic development, and the WTO for settlement of trade disputes.

There are countless historical events that have geoeconomic implications. Several of them, selected from a relatively recent period, are listed below for illustration:

- In addition to territorial occupations, Japan exploited Korea, China, and countries in Southeast Asia during World War II in order to satisfy needs for energy, raw materials, and food. The desire to imitate earlier European colonialism was also a motivating factor.
- Disputes between Japan and China regarding Daowidao (Senkaku in Japanese) are not only limited to territorial issues. Resources under the ocean in that region are the underlying economic interests. A similar problem emerged between Japan and Korea in connection with Dokdo (Takeshima). These disputes are not justified without Japanese imperialism and territorial expansions, for economic interests, during the "period of Japanese expansion" during the late nineteenth century through the early twentieth century.[14]
- The United States has interests in trade with China, Japan, Korea, and many emerging countries in the Asian Pacific region. As China rises as a new superpower and Russia has an access to the Pacific Ocean, this region has become strategically important to the United States.

There are also views supporting the geoeconomic perspectives addressed in this book:

- In his book (2002), Professor Joseph Stiglitz, Nobel Laureate in Economics Sciences in 2001, argued about the global financial crisis in 1970 by suggesting that "the countries in East Asia had no need for additional capital, given their high savings rate." He asserted that capital account liberalization pushed on these countries in the late

1980s and early 1990s by the U.S. Treasury Department in concert with the IMF was the single most important factor leading to the crisis.[15]

- In his book (2007), Alan Greenspan, former chairman of the Federal Reserve Board (1987–2006) stated: "I am saddened that it is politically inconvenient to acknowledge what everyone knows: the Iraq war is largely about oil."[16]

The data required to conduct research on geoeconomic areas are severely limited. They are often unavailable or inaccessible to academic researchers. In particular, many political events in many countries are not described in public records and thus seem mysterious. Differences in economic and political interests among countries increase the complexity in relationships between GEDs and GHEs. Fortunately, many cases are verifiable on the basis of economic principles along with natural laws.

1.4 GLOBAL ECONOMIC EFFICIENCY AND STABILITY

Geoeconomic inquiry into the political economy–oriented world of the twenty-first century is essential in pursuit of global economic efficiency and stability for leading countries, especially superpowers because of their powerful influence on the global economy. Their political and economic interests are largely consistent with one another's. Foreign policies in a country are designed to support its economic goal in the international markets. In pursuit of self-interests, however, the country in the face of global economic disparity is often motivated to generate any global event, that is, a GHE.

Given the causal connections between the GEDs and GHEs as focused on in this chapter, global economic efficiency and stability require rebalancing of global imbalances among countries or any type of regional or continental economic arrangements for fair competition among superpowers in the world market.[17] An effective way to achieve such a goal is their coherent policy responses to global economic problems rather than their power plays through international organizations as their political instruments. The conventional trade policy for free trade or fair trade is necessary but insufficient. This book proposes the global economy multipolarized by a *larger* number of superpowers, as addressed in sections 2.4 and 2.5 in chapter 3.

NOTES

1. The time path of adjustment process of an economic variable to the equilibrium is a serious subject in dynamic economics. It is concerned with a pattern of the time path of the equilibrium, whether the path is explosive or damp and oscillatory or nonoscillatory with certain degrees of amplitudes and durations of a series of the cycle

from an equilibrium state to another over time. Economists employ a difference or differential equation of a first-order or higher-order of a single equation or a system of simultaneous equations. This book is not concerned with a dynamic path but comparative static process.

2. The law of comparative advantage is a common proposition of classical, neoclassical, and modern theories, often referred to as the "Heckscher-Ohlin-Samuelson" (HOS) theory. It presupposes perfect competition for inter-industry trade. There are views suggesting intra-industry trade in the real world market that is monopolistically competitive or oligopolistic. See Krugman (1996) and Chung (2006).

3. Geoeconomics is a study that focuses on economic conditions or policies that are international in scope. As a branch of geopolitics, it is an interdisciplinary field that studies specifically the influences of politics, geography, history, and demography. Geopolitics was introduced by Friedrich Ratzel (1844–1904), a German geographer, and Rudolf Kjellen (1864–1922), a Swedish political scientist. Geoeconomics is attributed to Edward Luttwak (1942–), an American geopolitical economist, and Pascal Lorot (unavailable), a French geopolitical economist. Both geopolitics and geoeconomics are often misunderstood as the areas that study foreign policies of superpowers to expand their political and military influences on other superpowers and the colonialism of advanced countries in pursuit of expansions of their markets in underdeveloped countries for more exports of their products and imports of raw materials. This book does not address military or national security issues and the colonialism-related aspects.

4. The factor-price equalization theorem, a subset of the HOS theory, suggests that free trade equalizes prices of factors across the countries in the longrun and thus affects prices, foreign exchange rates, and the financial sector in the equalization process.

5. Stored magma-seismic vibrations and massive debts-financial crisis are a phenomenal comparison. Their scales and magnitudes are irrelevant to be discussed here.

6. The GED may be conceptualized in terms of statistical dispersions such as standard deviation (squared roots of variance) and the Gini coefficient that is mathematically based on the Lorenz curve.

7. There are many economic indicators that measure the relative economic situations of countries or groups of countries. Included are productions of manufacturing goods, hourly compensation, foreign reserve assets, and factor endowments such as human capital. Of course, they are not always consistent with each other.

8. Most of the historical events listed in this table are based on Barraclough (1997) and Roberts (2002).

9. Geographical explorations and industrial revolutions are the origin of the European dynamics for territorial expansions in Asia and Africa.

10. See Chung (2006).

11. There are three different states of industrial revolutions characterized as: The first industrial revolution was the mechanization of industry/factory (the mid-eighteenth century) in England; the second revolution was the automated assembly line, that is, the conveyer system for mass production (the early-twentieth century) in America. The third revolution is the digitization of manufacturing processes for customized mass production with less labor and labor cost and new materials by means of automated new processors like 3D printers. See *The Economist* (2012) for 3D, pp. 3–20.

12. See Roberts (2002), pp. 720–44 and p. 795.

13. See Chung (2006), pp. 14–21.

14. See Roberts (2002), pp.831–60.

15. Stiglitz, Joseph E. (2002), p. 99.

16. Greenspan, Alan (2007), p. 463.

17. Acemoglu and Robinson (2012) discuss why nations fall in their book. They suggest the "inclusive system" that ensures fair returns in all sectors. The inclusive system is largely consistent with a system of perfect competition in economics because three different kinds of competition in economic, political, and social areas can be condensed into a comprehensive term, "competition."

TWO

The Global Economy and Superpowers

Countless global events have occurred throughout history. Major historical events are mostly the outcomes of games played between or among
superpowers. If the global economy experiences a serious economic disparity (GED), conflicts of economic interest among superpowers may
drive the entire world into a political or economic crisis. In addition to
direct effects of the crisis on superpowers, there are also indirect effects
on smaller countries. In the case of large-scale turmoil, values are often
dictated by the survival instinct of human beings. In such circumstances,
our world is not so different from the animal kingdom.[1] It is indeed a
stage for superpowers' games.

Given the size of the world economy at a certain time, the objective of
a superpower is to maximize its share of the world economic pie at the
expense of one or more superpowers. The economic behavior of superpowers A and B is illustrated by the Cournot theory of oligopoly. It
assumes mutual interdependence between oligopolists. Equilibrium outputs for oligopolists A and B are determined at the intersection point of
their reaction functions. The equilibrium point in the Cournot model corresponds to the Nash equilibrium in game theory, which is a systematic
way of choosing the optimum strategy in a situation of both conflicting
and parallel interests through international political interactions.

The interactive economic behavior of oligopolists A and B is applicable to international strategy behavior of countries A and B as economic
oligarchs. They have an economic interest in maximizing international
market shares that simultaneously determine their global political power.[2] The strategy pair finally achieved by the two countries, "Agree,
Agree," is referred to as the Nash solution for the particular international
issue equivalent to equilibrium (if country A's choice is optimal, given

17

B's choice, and B's choice is optimal, given A's choice). In terms of politics, this situation corresponds to a peacetime period, when political stability between A and B revitalizes international trade and ensures economic prosperity in the world. In reality, however, conflicts of economic or political interest between and among countries are not easily reconciled and thus yield geopolitically sensitive countries and regions.

This chapter explores superpowers' behavior that is primarily based on their economic and political interests. There are economic superpowers, exemplified by G-7 (Canada, France, Germany, Italy, Japan, the U.K., and the United States) and other newly developed countries (China and South Korea). The IMF quota that determines the voting power of a member country is another reasonable criterion to identify superpowers. The United States has about 20 percent whereas other superpowers have about 5–7 percent on the average. There are also political superpowers. They are the five permanent members in the United Nations Security Council (China, France, Russian Federation, the United Kingdom, and the United States) of fifteen current members including nonpermanent members. This book considers superpowers comprehensibly. They are the countries listed above, in either the political category or the economic category.

2.1 SUPERPOWERS' INTERESTS

There are countries and geographical areas in the world where conflicts of economic
and/or political interest among superpowers frequently prevail. Without special information, any person interested in geography and world history can identify them from a world atlas. They are reportedly the regions that U.S. naval bases cover around the world: the Atlantic Ocean and Western Europe, the Pacific Ocean, East Asia, the Mediterranean area, and Eastern Europe, and the Middle East and Indian Ocean.

Countries where food, minerals, and oil are produced and ports, canals, bays, and straits where cargo ships transport them are especially appealing to superpowers. As indicated in the previous chapter, Germany attacked the Caucasus during World War II to secure oil fields and food. Japan invaded Indonesia for similar reasons and attacked Pearl Harbor to prevent U.S. intervention. The Gulf War of 1990s was influenced by oil resources in the Middle East. Today, China secures raw materials almost everywhere in the world. It is impossible to imagine a world independent of superpowers' interests.

A limited number of sample countries/regions and facilities are presented here to illustrate what and where superpowers' interests are:

1. Afghanistan

Afghanistan is a landlocked country that borders Pakistan, Iran, Turkmenistan, Uzbekistan, Tajikistan, and China. Afghanistan is strategically important because the country has an access to the oil-rich Persian Gulf. The Soviet Union invaded Afghanistan in December 1975 and controlled it for about ten years. The United States has actively fought in Afghanistan since 2001.

2. South China Sea

China claims several islands in the East China Sea and South China Sea as part of the so-called lost territories. The territorial claims by China are related to its interest in large oil deposits and mineral resources under the sea in this vast area. Advancement of China and Russia to these two seas is in conflict with U.S. interests in the Pacific region. The South China Sea is crucial to Japan and South Korea for transportation of oil from the Middle East. In addition to a strategy for counter-balancing the political influence of China in Asia, the United States has its economic interests through various free trade agreements and regional groups such as ASEAN, ASEAN+3, EAS, and APEC.[3] Given all kinds of strategic scenarios involving the United States, including a naval blockade at the Straits of Malacca, China would try to secure every regional source of oil and natural gas in Asia.

3. Korean Peninsula

The Korean peninsula is a strategic crossroads for the superpowers China, Japan, Russia, and the United States. As a rim land of the southeast Pacific Ocean, the sea routes around the peninsula are geopolitically important in the Far East. As a member of the OECD and one of most rapidly growing countries, South Korea is very important for the world economy, especially in terms of international trade.

4. Middle Eastern Region

Major oil-producing countries are in this region. They are crucial to oil-consuming nations, including the United States. The entire region has become strategically sensitive, especially since the 1970s.

5. Panama Canal

The Panama Canal connects the Atlantic and Pacific Oceans. It is a key conduit for maritime trade between not only the east and west coasts of North America and South America but also intercontinental transportation between Asia and America.

6. Strait of Malacca

The Strait of Malacca is the narrow shipping lane, approximately 500 miles long, between the Peninsula of Malaysia and Sumatra of Indonesia. It links the Indian Ocean and Pacific Ocean. It is estimated that about one-quarter of the world's traded goods, including oil, are transported through this channel for Japan, China, Korea, and other emerging countries in Asia.

7. Suez Canal

The Suez Canal linking the Mediterranean, the Red Sea, and the India Ocean is critical for trade between Asia and Europe. The canal reduces the total miles by 2,700 for transporting crude oil from Saudi Arabia to the United States. Over 20,000 vessels pass through the canal per year.

8. Turkey

Turkey, a bicontinental Eurasian country, is geopolitically important. The country borders Europe, the Middle East, and the Caucasus. Most important of all, Turkey controls the entry to and exit from the Black Sea, where the political unrest in Ukraine prevails at present. It is the only exit for Eastern European countries, Central Asian countries, and Russia from the Mediterranean Ocean. During World War I, one of the top political and military strategies of England, in concert with France, was to block Russian advancement to the Mediterranean Sea. The Baku-Tbilisi-Ceyhan pipeline is an energy conduit to the Mediterranean area.

We now turn our attention to events (GHEs). They can be divided into three different subperiods. Note that the post-World War period includes GHEs during the post-World War I, followed by GHEs during the post-World War II.

1. The Period of European Expansions in the Eighteenth–Nineteenth Centuries

- Britain ruled India, took a fifty-year leasehold of Hong Kong following the opium war in China, and colonized America.
- France occupied nine African countries and formed the franc zone with those countries.
- Spain took the Philippines in 1560. The United States took the Philippines from Spain in 1898.

2. The Period of World War II

- Germany attacked Soviet Russia to secure oil from the Caucasus region.

- Japan occupied countries in the Far East and southeast Asia during World War II. Japan, an island country with few natural resources and food sources, invaded them for desperately needed energy and raw materials.

3. The Post–World War Period

Key events in international economic history are listed below:

1880–1914: Gold standard

1914–1918: World War I

1918–1939: Gold standard returned in the United States (1919) and the U.K. (1925) and abandoned in the U.K. (1931) and United States (1933)

Great Depression (1929–1939)

1939–1945: World War II

Bretton Woods Conference in July 1944 where IMF and World Bank were established

1945–1970: The period of fixed exchange regime

GATT established in 1947

EU formed from 1957–1970

1971–1973: Smithsonian Agreement in December 1971

1974–1979: Oil crises in 1974 and 1978

European Monetary System established in March 1979

1985–: Plaza Agreement of the G-5 in September 1985

Uruguay Round Agreement in 1986 and WTO established

Stock market crash in 1987

NAFTA in 1993

International Financial Crises: Mexico (1994–1995), Brazil (1999), and Argentina

(2001–2002); Asia (1997–1998) in Thailand, Malaysia, Indonesia, and South Korea

1998: European Central Bank formed in June

1999: Euro (€) created in June

2001–: Doha Round for multilateral trade negotiations after the Uruguay Round

2008–: Global Financial Crisis in the United States in 2008 and contagion to euro countries.

2014: Emergence of the United States as a major energy producer and its impact on the global energy market, including the Russian economy and OPEC.

Note that the GHEs presented above are mostly geoeconomic events initiated by superpowers. They confirm that most international organizations or institutions are basically forums for superpowers.

2.2 EMERGENCE OF CHINA'S ECONOMY

In today's dynamic world of global politics and economics, nothing is stationary. China has recently emerged as a superpower. The emergence of China as a superpower is significant because its omnipresence on the world stage signals a paradigm shift in the existing global structure of economy and politics.

Overall, China has been growing rapidly since the 1980s under the open-door policy of the Deng Xiaoping regime. The low-wage economy of China (population 1.4 billion), boosted by massive investment and technology transfers by multinational corporations, has grown rapidly since 2004 at double-digit rates for certain time periods. China's economy has stayed strong in global economic stagnation today and is an economic powerhouse in the world as the second largest economy in the world, next to the U.S. economy of about a 15 trillion dollar GDP. Although it is slowing down now, China still grows at 7–8 percent per year and is expected to grow during most of the twenty-first century. Table 2.1 exhibits data relevant to this and subsequent sections.

China has come a long way to achieve superpower status. As China's trade surplus has steadily increased since the early 1970s, the United States has tried to open the market in China for U.S. exports and to realign the exchange rate between the dollar and the undervalued yuan.

By definition, economics is a main component of geoeconomics. One can confirm the essential role of economics from U.S. foreign policy for the past seventy years. The latter has been oriented by economic interests reflected in U.S. trade policy. Geoeconomic insights into actual trade practices between the two countries help us understand the objective of U.S. trade policy toward China. The United States tried to reform China's economy and *contain* it as an integral part of the competitive world economy. U.S. trade policy is for coordinated application of bilateral, regional, and multilateral trade agreements. In this set of three-tier trade policies, any geoeconomic interests in a specific issue with a particular country are reflected in bilateral trade agreements.[4] Specific U.S. policies to attain the objective were:

- Bipartisan support for market opening by lifting of the trade embargo in 1972
- Bilateral Commercial Agreement in 1980
- A large number of specific bilateral agreements mostly in the 1990s[5]
- Strenuous efforts to appreciate the value of the yuan

After intense negotiations over a decade between the United States and China, bilateral agreements were concluded in November 1999. After the

Table 2.1.   GDP, International Reserves by Area, and U.S. Exports and Imports

	GDP[a]	International Reserves[b]	U.S. Trade by Area[c] Exports	U.S. Trade by Area[c] Imports
OECD				
U.S.	13,595.6	88.0		
EU[d]	13,831.7			
Asia[e]	5,277.7			
OECD total	37,794.8			
Asian Countries				
Japan	3,954.8	820.4		
Korea	1,322.9	198.2		
China	9,124.2	2,087.3		
India	3,458.2[f]	177.3		
Indonesia	930.7			
Total	18,790.8			
Europe		567.0	335.4	453.6
Asia and Pacific			418.1	8I8.9
Other				
Brazil			228.2	

Notes:
   [a]billions of dollars, 2010, constant prices, OECD base year
   [b]billions of SDR, 2011, end of period, international reserves consist of monetary authorities' holdings of gold (at SDR 35 per ounce), SDRs, reserve positions at the IMD, and foreign exchange.
   [c]billions of dollars
   [d]27 member countries
   [e]Japan and Korea, two Asian OECD members and selected countries
   [f]2009
   Data: OECD, *OECD Factbook*, 2013.

agreements to reduce tariff and nontariff barriers to U.S. exports of industrial goods and agricultural products and services, the United States endorsed China's accession to the WTO. Since China became a member of the WTO in 2001, its exports have increased dramatically, catalyzing the entire economy toward an unprecedented peak. The enormous amounts of trade surplus in China and its foreign exchange holdings, including U.S. Treasury bills and bonds, became enough to shake the world economy. As one of the most powerful countries in terms of economic size and political influence in the world, many analysts think that China will outpace the size of the U.S. economy by 2050.[6]

The world itself is a closed economy. The total amount of trade deficits of all trade-deficit countries (for example, the West) equals the total amount of trade surplus of all trade-surplus countries (the East). Specifically, the principle of accounting balance suggests that a change in the total surplus of China, India, and other emerging Asian countries is equivalent, *ceteris paribus*, to a change in total claims of the East on the West.[7] Such a reversal phenomenon, observed long after the hemispheric economic disparity against the East in the past, is largely consistent with the Heckscher-Ohlin-Samuelson theory (HOS), the modern theory of international trade based on different factor endowments and intensities. In accordance with the factor-price equalization theorem, a subset of the HOS, prices of factors are equalized in the long run, probably after alternating waves of factor prices that will continue until the equalization of prices of productive factors is completed (between, i.e., the East and West).[8]

Will the overall difference in economic growth between rapidly growing countries and matured economies continue in the future? It is reasonable to expect that the economies of advanced countries will be sluggish in growth. The U.S. economy has barely been sustained by the Fed's QE (quantitative easing) policy.[9] Given massive debt, the fiscal cliff, and the recent U.S. verge toward national default, it is uncertain that the U.S. economy will keep its position as the largest economy in the world. Except for Germany, the euro zone economy is also experiencing financial crisis. The Japanese economy is far from recovery.[10] It is attempting to recover its economy through a policy of virtually infinite money supply (initially 20 trillion yen) that is similar to the Fed's QE.

China and India, two of the fastest growing countries in the world, should continue to grow throughout the twenty-first century. As of September 2013, China holds substantial foreign reserves (3,660 billion dollars) and U.S. Treasury securities invested (1,280 billion dollars). There are views in China that

(1) China should reduce its U.S. Treasury securities to avoid the financial risk of a tapering off of U.S. QE policy;

(2) The role of the U.S. dollar as the key currency is questionable. A new currency system should be established with a new key currency.

These views seem reasonable but premature. Does China have any other alternatives at this time?

- These views ignore global economic repercussions. At present, China's export-oriented economy is slowing down because the global economy is sluggish. If China reduces its investment in U.S. Treasury securities, U.S. imports from China will decrease. China's GDP is huge, but per capita income is still low. Given the enormous population, there are many socioeconomic problems. U.S. public debt is mostly to its domestic sector. Reportedly, China's holdings of U.S. securities are less than 10 percent of the total.
- The yuan has constantly been under pressure for appreciation, especially from the United States, even before the 2008 financial crises in the United States and Europe. Since the financial crisis in Greece, the euro has depreciated with respect to the yuan by 15, which will, in turn, affect the exchange rate between the dollar and yuan and indirectly the exchange rate between the euro and the dollar. Yuen has increasingly been important as a major international currency. The number of countries and areas that settle the trade balances in yuan has steadily increased and is over 200 at present. The two central banks of China and EU have made the agreement for currency swaps between the yuan and the euro. However, the yuan is not ready to be the key global currency mainly because its mobility is subject to governmental controls.

China also has many internal problems. Specifically, they are as follows:

- While the scale of its manufacturing sector is large, it is not strong enough in terms of international competitiveness in the absence of the investment and technology of multinational corporations.
- Although currently making some efforts in this direction, China's technology needs to become more innovative in order to maintain high economic growth in the future.
- As wages increase rapidly, the comparative advantage of a large population diminishes.
- Fast growth causes serious environmental problems.
- The distribution of income is seriously biased, resulting in a significant gap between rich and poor. The middle income bracket is thin. A considerable gap between the existing upper class and the lower income brackets jeopardizes political stability.
- Rapid urbanization in certain areas and cities results in social "safety net" problems in housing, education, medical facilities, transportation, jobs, and corruption and crime prevention.
- Domestic consumption is not currently strong enough to replace export-led growth.

These problems are not unique to China. They are commonly observed in India, Brazil, and other emerging countries and also observed in developed countries. Overall, however, emergence of China's economy is expected to continue gradually in the future.

2.3 PARADIGM SHIFTS IN THE WORLD ECONOMY

A question arises: What is the significance of the global emergence of China's economy? The answer to this question depends on how one would look at it, positively or negatively. Given current trends in the world economy, there will be a significant transfer of global wealth from the Western to the Eastern hemisphere, reportedly by 2025. This transfer of wealth will likely restructure the world economy from the bipolar economies of the United States and the EU to a tripolar system. Such a result has important geoeconomic implications. The international market share of a country generally determines its global economic power, which determines, in turn, the global political power of the country. Indeed, political power within the international community requires economic power tantamount to political power. In other words, the global political position of a country and its economic power are proportional, and the former in the absence of the latter is meaningless. Also, no country would pursue political power in the absence of economic interests or gains. The correlation between economic power and political power implies that political superpowers are economic superpowers and *vice versa*. In pursuit of local political power, therefore, the first priority of foreign policy strategy in each country is to maximize its economic power and thus economic interests. A good example is China today. As the global economic power of China comes to exceed that of Russia, China has seemingly replaced Russia as one of two big superpowers in international political forums.

History suggests that there have been alternating waves of rise and fall in national economies throughout history. Except for the Silk Road trade in ancient times, followed by trade and travel opened by Mongols (1279–1368), China was hermetic at the time of Marco Polo's journey to China (1271–1295) and during the period from the early fifteenth to nineteenth century. Now, China has emerged as the country with the second largest economy.[11] Although the potential future growth of an economy with a population of 1.4 billion in the future is enormous, China still has a long way to go—quantitatively as well as qualitatively—to match the economies in the Western hemisphere. Actual growth in the future depends on a wide range of economic as well as political factors: investment, both domestic and foreign, quality of labor as determined by education and training, attitude toward work, capacity for innovation, lifestyles, social justice, international political stability, and so on, are just some of factors that will determine China's future on the world stage. Readers can refer to human capital, discussed in chapter 6 of this book. Contrary to its initial growth momentum, China's economy is now slowing down. Both the IMF and the World Bank warn about a hard landing, although Chinese authorities respond that the rate of growth was above 8 percent in 2013.

The basic propositions on China's economy maintained in this book are as follows:

- The economic growth of China has decoupled the shares of the world's economic pie dominated by the United States and Europe.
- The current financial crises in the United States and Europe are attributable partly to emerging economies in Asia, including China, and thus may be viewed as a process of adjustment of economic disparities to the global equilibrium.
- China's economic growth is not gravity defying and parallels the natural law on waves in the ocean that undulate in all directions.
- In the future, there will eventually be a wave that reverses the current tide of world economic trends.

Overall, China's economy has been growing rapidly for three decades. However, China has only just started to become a real superpower; sustained growth will be required in the future.

2.4 A MULTIPOLAR WORLD ECONOMY

Before World War I, Europe was the center of international politics and economy. The industrial revolutions of the eighteenth–nineteenth centuries in Britain were the driving forces for industrialization in all of Europe. The first industrial revolution (1760–1820) in England pushed it to the forefront of the world economy. The second industrial revolution (1870–1914) took place in several other European countries. The industrial revolutions enabled mass production in Europe as a whole and required Europeans to find overseas markets to sell their products and to secure raw materials. During this period, there were many colonial discoveries, cessions, and annexations by European countries. For example, India (1805–1947), Africa (nineteenth century), Hong Kong after the Opium War (1839–1842), and North America (1607–1783) came under British control. However, successive wars destroyed human and material resources and ravaged European tradition and order. The age of European supremacy was over by the end of the period of the world wars. The United States participated in both wars. Except for the Pearl Harbor invasion, however, the infrastructure of the U.S. economy was virtually intact during World War II. After the war, the United States emerged as the politically and economically most powerful and prosperous country in the world. From such a vantage point, the United States has played the leading role on the global stage and contributed to world peace and economic development through this role.[12] During the Cold War period of political confrontation with Russia and China, the United States again became involved in wars in the Far East and Middle East. The *domino theory* of foreign policy reigned.

As discussed in the previous section, U.S. strategy in Asia is to embrace not only China but also other countries in East Asia. Such a policy is viewed as a preemptive strategy to minimize China's influence in this region and to isolate China by strengthening relations with reliable allies.[13] However, China has outpaced U. S. expectations. Despite backlash from political upheaval in 1989, the Asian economic crisis of 1997, and the financial crisis and its impact at present (2007–), China's economy has now surpassed the Japanese economy (although not in terms of per capita income) as the second largest in the world. With an annual average rate of economic growth over 10 percent during the period of 2004–2010 and low wages, China continued to maintain a relatively high rate of growth, over 8 percent, in 2011 and 2012. It is expected that China will keep a fast pace of growth and likely be the biggest creditor country of the United States through much of the twenty-first century. India, another populous country, with 1.34 billion people and an ample low-wage labor force, has achieved rapid economic growth based on a service sector that produces more than half of the country's GDP.

China has now emerged as a new superpower and this affects U.S. influence in Asia and its market share around the world. Geoeconomic competition between the United States and China is increasingly keen amid their conflicts of interest in the Pacific area at large. There are even territorial disputes between China and Japan, for example, over Daoidau (Senkaku) and between China and the Philippines. One can easily imagine geoeconomic scenarios about superpower strategies in this greater Asian region that could critically affect economies of Far Eastern countries. It could be a scenario that puts U.S. naval forces on a mission in the Strait of Malacca between the Andaman Sea and the South China Sea, the main shipping channel of oil from the Middle East to the Far East. A blockade of the channel for any political or military reason in the future would be detrimental to oil-consuming nations in the Far East. In response to the blockade, China would negotiate with an Indian Ocean country for establishment of a depository base of crude oil imported from the Middle East and minerals from Africa.

As a new superpower, China has now joined the United States and Europe (or EU), the two primary national entities as main actors on the world stage. According to OECD statistics, the average annual rate of GDP growth of China for 2004–2010 was 11.1 percent. Many countries in the Far East are concerned about dramatic increases in China's defense spending. As the size of the economy in a country increases, it is natural to expect that spending for national defense in that country increases proportionally. In economics, however, public goods are characterized as non-rival in consumption and non-exclusive in benefit (irrespective of payment) and thus result in market failure. No country can afford to spend its budget indefinitely on public goods. In comparison with defense spending in other advanced countries, the GDP share of the budget for national defense in China is within the range of 2–4.5 percent for those countries that allocate relatively more for military spending.[14]

What is the significance of China's emergence? There has been a widespread notion that the West was the benefactor whereas the East was the beneficiary. However, the Asian economy (China, India, Japan, and other fast growing countries such as South Korea) has grown sufficiently into a powerful economic region.[15] Emergence of the Asian economy is meaningful as an entity from the perspective of *social justice*, implying that, in accordance with Professor Friedrich Hayek, a Nobel Laureate in Economics (1976), it has come out largely through the competitive world market instead of through a simple redistribution of global income.[16] The Asian region has become symbolically a third axis supporting the world economy after Europe (before World War I) and the United States (after World War II). As the East Asian economy takes a greater part in the world economy, its political weight has also grown significantly to make a contribution to the resilience of the world. The system of tripolar axes should stabilize the world economy more firmly through trilateral relationships than the bipolar system or unipolar system. Such a paradigm shift of the global economy may be viewed as a natural consequence after the economy-wide disparity of the East relative to the West. The global economic disparity (GED) has gradually energized Asian countries to grow toward a global equilibrium. The underlying rationale here is similar to the second law of thermodynamics (about heat flowing from a hot to a cool object toward equilibrium) or to Newton's law of universal gravitation (about any two objects of mass attracting each other). However, the global equilibrium is constantly disturbed by exogenous shocks such as political and economic crises and technological innovations. They form alternating waves of the world economy moving in a circular fashion in the long run.

In Principles of Economics class, students learn that, in the absence of entry into the market by the potential competitors, the (existing) monopolist produces less and charges more than competitive producers. The theory of competition suggests that economic efficiency is ensured under an open, flexible, self-adjusting, competitive economy of a large number of firms. Trilateral competition results in more efficiency in the global economy than bilateral competition does. In accordance with international trade theory, multilateral competition increases global welfare and economic efficiency under free trade. The rationale here is mutual gain for both China and all other countries trading with China. The theory of portfolio selection in finance is the basis for investment. It suggests that investors should diversify their portfolios to minimize risk, implying that diversification maximizes their financial stability.[17] The world should be economically and politically more stable under trilateral relationships among superpowers than under conventional bilateral relationships. Apart from political and ideological issues, this rationale implies that a multipolar system of China-the EU-the United States reduces global economic disparities and alleviates the welfare losses from world dominance by a single superpower or two. Conflicts of economic and political interest among a limited number of superpowers preoccupied by historically negative ways of thinking are a major barrier to greater prosperity for the entire world. Nothing is wrong with China's export of goods and services to the rest of the world at lower prices. If China's emergence is *positively* viewed, its contributions to the world are potentially enormous. Of course, it is important for China to partake in the world economy as a fair and mature economic partner. In addition to preferential choices of portfolio investment and holding massive amounts of foreign reserves, a greater flexibility of the yuan in accordance with competitive foreign exchange markets and foreign direct investment are expected by the rest of the world.

The global economic disparity (GED), including poverty in the world, is too big and serious to be dealt with by one or two superpowers. Additional regional economic cooperation is desirable for balancing global economic disparities that would otherwise generate major historical crises. The WTO encourages regional free trade agreements on the grounds that interregional arrangements are consistent with the spirit of competitive trade.[18] The United States considers the APEC important for U.S. engagement in the Asia-Pacific region and is now pushing for the Trans-Pacific Partnership (TPP) of twelve countries as the primary vehicle for economic cooperation in the future. In addition, the APEC-Transatlantic linkage motivated the EU to create a forum between Asia and Europe. The ASEM (Asia-Europe Meeting), initiated in Thailand in 1996, is an informal dialogue channel of thirteen Asian countries, EU member states, and the European Commission.

Waves alternating between the rise and fall of a national/global economy are similar to phenomena dictated by natural law. An equilibrium or disequilibrium situation cannot be perpetuated. The economic growth of China (and other fast growing economies in Asia) has decoupled the economic growth of the United States (and Europe), which will predictably be likely reversed in the future. Contrary to what economics manifests, however, global disequilibrium rebounds due to random shocks generated anywhere in the world, and such a reverse often leads to crises. The economic crises in the United States and Europe today are partly due to a greater share of the global economic pie now being taken by China and other fast growing Asian economies. In other words, greater shares taken by Europe and the United States in the past have resulted in global economic disparity for many generations. This is not to blame a dynamic West in the past half millennium but to suggest that a static East was primarily responsible.

Hemispheric adjustments of the global economy through fair competition in the global market and harmonious reconciliation of races, religious, and political convictions ensure political peace in the world. The expanded size of world economy would significantly enhance this. Balanced growth of the world economy under the fair market competition is essential for political stability. In conclusion, the world should move in a process of adjustment toward global equilibrium in the long run and move in the direction warranted by economic and political rationale.

2.5 SIGNIFICANCE OF EMERGING COUNTRIES IN THE WORLD MARKET

The economic size of each emerging country is small. However, the aggregated size of their economies is significant enough to influence the global economy and politics. For example, no one would ever have imagined that South Korea, a part of the small country divided after 36 years of hardship from forced occupation by Japan and devastated during the Korean War (1950–1953), would become a member of the Organization for Economic Co-operation and Development (OECD, established in 1948, 34 developed member countries as of today). Other emerging countries have also performed remarkably. In *Economic Report of the President* (2011, p. 90), the Council of Economic Advisors suggests:

> The United States accounts for roughly one-quarter of the world economy, and consumption has historically accounted for roughly two-thirds of the U.S. economy. Thus, one might normally expect 17 (= 1/4 x 2/3) percent of world aggregate demand growth to come from U.S. consumers. But emerging and developing economies often grow faster than more mature economies. Thus, a larger portion of world growth would be expected to come from emerging economies, than their share of the world economy would warrant.

The OECD maintains close relations with Brazil, China, India, Indonesia, the Russian Federation and South Africa as potential members in the future. Table 2.2 exhibits growth rates of GDP and GDP per capita in current and constant prices for selected Asian countries, the EU and the United States, along with the OECD. The economies of emerging countries have grown strongly in comparison with advanced countries.

In terms of GDP per capita, as shown in figure 2.1 for (a) OECD countries including the U.S., EU27 and Japan, (b) China and India, and (c) countries

Table 2.2.   GDP Growth Rates and Per Capita GDP of Selected Countries (in percent of GDP per capita in U.S. dollars, current prices)

	Japan	Korea	U.S.	EU27	OECD	China	India	Indonesia
2000	5.7	10.3	5.4	18.5	6.1	0.1	0.0	9.1
2005	3.8	5.6	5.5	4.7	3.6	13.9	15.8	6.7
2010	5.3	7.1	3.3	2.3	3.3	10.3	10.0	4.8
In	Percent	Of	GDP	In	U.S.	Dollars,	Constant	Prices
2008	-1.0	2.3	-0.3	3.4		9.8	4.9	6.1
2009	-5.5	0.3	-2.8	-4.3		9.2	9.1	4.5
2010	4.7	6.4	2.5	2.1	3.0	10.5		6.2
2011	-1.0	3.7	1.9	1.6				
2012		2.1	2.8	-3.5				

Source: (1) OECD, *OECD Factbook*, 2013, p.35.

(2) U.S. Census Bureau, *Statistical Abstract of the United States*, 2012, p. 846.

in Africa and South Asia, there is an oblique fault among them. The fault would have been steeper without (b). The figure

illustrates graphically the actual case that countries in (b) have motivated themselves to grow in the face of global economic disparities (GEDs). South Korea went through a similar stage before it became a member of the OECD and evolves into another stage amid dynamic forces in super-powers' competition.

This section provides a rationale for a multipolar global economy that stabilizes the world economy. In the case of Asia, many countries have already participated in various regional arrangements. Forums such as the ASEAN (Association of Southeast Asian Nations), ASEAN+3 and the EAS (East Asian Summit) have facilitated rapid increases in intra-region-al trade and led to a regional economic integration of countries in Asia approaching to that of the EU. Included are Japan, Korea, and China, the three major countries trading heavily with the United States. The United States is particularly interested in rebalancing relationships with coun-tries in the Far East because they are not only important economic part-ners but also meet U.S. strategy for pivoting toward Asia. The recent free trade agreement between Korea and the United States is evidence for the

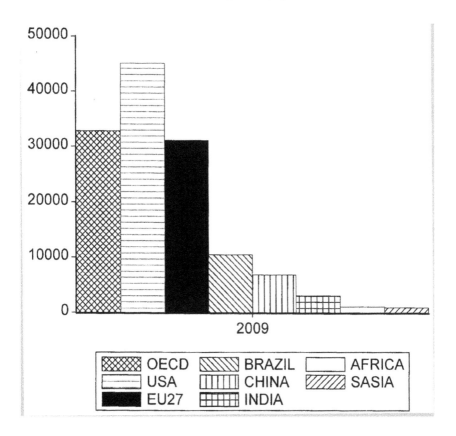

Figure 2.1. GDP per capita. Note: In percent of GDP per capita in U.S. dollars, current price. Gross National Income (GNI) for Africa and S. Asia available up to 2009 in data (2). Data: (1) OECD, Factbook, 2013, p. 35. (2) U.S. Census Bureau, Statistical Abstract of the United States, 2012, Washington, D.C.: U.S. GPO, p. 846.

mutual importance. Other economically significant countries in Asia are Singapore, Hong Kong, Taiwan, Thailand, Malaysia, and Indonesia. Clearly emerging Asian countries make an important contribution to the world economy, and the Asian economy as a whole becomes an important part of the multipolarization of the global economy.

Although the South (or Latin) American economy has not yet drawn much global attention, it includes rapidly growing countries such as Brazil and Chile. The OECD maintains close relations with these countries. South (or Latin) America has abundant natural resources and oil. Over the course of the last decade, South America has achieved substantial economic growth and made significant progress in reducing poverty. Unlike most Asian countries, South American nations have additional advantages. They largely share a common culture and religion and speak only two languages. The South American economy will likely arise as another important regional economic entity and will enhance the likelihood of success, together with Argentina (relieved in the future of its default on 29 billion dollars in debt reported as of August 1, 2014) and Venezuela, a member of the OPEC.

The Asian economic region, South American economic region along with the existing European economic region (already existing in the form of the EU), and North American Economic region (already existing in the form of NAFTA) are the four regional economic entities that would constitute an ideal commonwealth for the global economy beyond the current system of the limited number of regional economic integrations. They are the model proposed here for the stabilization and prosperity of the world economy through intra- and inter-regional competitions and cooperation.

In conclusion, causal relationships between GEDs and GHEs are principally superpower phenomena. Economic and/or political interests motivate superpowers to conduct influential geoeconomic activities throughout the world. The world was under a bipolar system—the United States and the EU—during the post–World War II period. Except for Japan, though currently dysfunctional as an advanced economy, Asia did not play a significant role until China emerged as a superpower around the end of the twentieth century, apparently to be followed by India. Contributions made by emerging countries in Asia are increasingly significant today. As a group, the Asian economy is an important part of the world economy. It is now South America's turn to demonstrate its capacity as the fourth axis of the global economy. Economists believe in the principle of economic efficiency under perfect competition: more output and lower price. Removing global economic disparities throughout the world is consistent with the theory of perfect competition. A multipolar system will make the world more competitive, minimize superpower hegemony, and ameliorate poverty in the third world through their more effective coordination and cooperation. Free trade within the GATT-WTO framework is important but insufficient to turn the global economy competitive. It is desirable for the global community including international institutions to support the South American region so that it can emerge as the fourth axis of the global economy.

NOTES

1. This view does not implicitly address colonialism. Atrocities and persecutions under colonialism in the past do not exist in the world today.

2. See Chung (1991) for the rationale for global economic power of a country that is proportional to its international market share. This paper finds the effect of international market shares on the global economic power of each of the seven major industrial countries. Given the positive correlation between economic power and political

power, the larger the market share in the world market of a country, the stronger the political power of the country.

3. Regional economic integrations in Asia include:

ASEAN (Association of South East Asian Nations, established in 1967 in Bangkok) =
10 member countries that include Indonesia, Malaysia, Philippines, Singapore and Thailand (5 original members above), Brunei Darussalam (1984), Vietnam (1995), Lao PDR and Myanmar (1997), and Cambodia (1999);
ASEAN+3 = 13 member countries; 10 ASEAN countries plus China, Japan, and South Korea
EAS (East Asia Summit) = 16 member countries; ASEAN+3 plus Australia, India, and New Zealand;
APEC (Asian Pacific Economic Cooperation) = 22 member countries; EAS excluding
India, Russia, Taiwan, Chile, Peru, Mexico, the U.S. and Canada;
FTAs (Free Trade Agreements) of the U.S. with Asian countries.

4. See Chung (2006), p. 65.

5. Included are agreements on intellectual property rights in 1995 and 1996, agreements on textiles in 1994 and 1997 that reduced China's exports to the United States, and the agreement on agricultural cooperation. See Chung (2006), pp. 82–86.

6. Per capita income of China is still very low. According to the OECD, it was $7,519 in 2010 as opposed to $33,785 in the same year in Japan. See table 1.1 in chapter 1. The United States attempted to keep China within the multilateral trade framework. The U.S. *containment policy* was the U.S. foreign policy to maintain the balance of power between the United States and the USSR after World War II. It was suggested by George F. Kennan, the U.S. ambassador to the Soviet Union (1904–2005). See George F. Kennan, Long Telegram and the Sources of Soviet Conduct, "X" "Sources of Soviet Conduct," *Foreign Affairs*, XXV, pp. 575–76. Also see Kissinger, Henry, *Diplomacy*, (1994), Chapter 28, p. 723.

7. India is also emerging as another superpower. While China's is based on low-wage manufacturing industry, India's economy is based on the service industry. It is also notable that the total population of India (1.2 billion) is slightly less than that of China (1.4 billion) as of September 2013.

8. There are three different sets of trade theories: classical theory (often referred to as Ricardian law of comparative advantage), neoclassical theory, and modern theory (referred to as the Heckscher-Ohlin-Samuelson theory). The modern theory is based on two fundamental concepts: factor endowment (e.g., capital and labor) and factor intensity in two different countries. The theory suggests that a factor-abundant country exports the factor-intensive good.

9. Chapter 4 discusses quantitative easing (QE) in detail.

10. Since the oil crises in the 1970s, the U.S. economy has continued to decline. Japan was the largest trading partner as well as the major competitor to the United States. U.S. trade deficits increased. Japanese investors purchased real estate, from golf courses on the West Coast to Rockefeller Center on the East Coast. However, the Japanese economy began to show the structural problems in banking and weaknesses in their leading export industries, high technology, and automobiles, in the face of strong competitions of rapidly growing countries in the Far East.

11. See Ferguson (2011) on this view.

12. The United States played important roles in the process of forming international organizations such as the United Nations, the IMF, the World Bank, GATT/WTO, regional trade agreement such as the NAFTA, and countless bilateral agreements. For the global events during the post–World War II period , see section 2.1 of this chapter.

13. The countries that the United States counts on its side include Japan, South Korea, India, Australia, Indonesia, and Vietnam. See Twining (2007). In addition, the United States has maintained diplomatic ties and established strong defense coopera-

tion for two decades with Mongolia, a strategically important country landlocked by Russia and China. See Freeman and Kral (2007).

14. In general, military expenditures in Middle Eastern countries are higher than in countries in other areas: U.S. (4.1), China (4.3), India (2.5), UK (2.4) Korea, S. (2.7). See Bureau of the Census, *Statistical Abstract of the United States*, 2012, p. 876. Also see *Stockholm International Peace Research Institute Yearbook* (SIPRI), 2013.

15. *Region* is a general, comprehensive term here. It should not be construed as any kind of trade union corresponding. There are several different kinds of economic integration: free trade area where member countries remove all trade barriers among themselves but keep individual trade barriers against nonmember countries; customs union that requires member countries to remove all trade barriers among themselves and to adopt a common set of trade barriers against nonmember countries; common market where members allow free mobility of factors in addition to what free trade area allows to do for members.

16. For *social justice,* see Hayek (1976).

17. This book is not a quantitative study. However, it would be helpful for readers to conceptualize the propositions in terms of the mean-variance analysis in the statistical approach to asset market. This approach views that the total risk of portfolio is a function of variability (variance or $\sigma 2$) of the return of an asset from its average (mean or μ) return, variability of another asset, and the correlations between the two stochastic variables (covariance or cov). Among the three possibilities for estimated values of the covariance, the case of a negative covariance ($cov < 0$) contributes to reduce the overall portfolio variance or risk. See Melvin (2004, pp. 109–13) for the approach to portfolio diversification.

18. See Chung (2006) on the WTO articles.

II

Disparities in International Trade and Finance

THREE

Open Economy Macroeconomic Principles and Policy Implications

The global economy has frequently experienced economic crises since World War II. The primary cause of the crises in an area is the economic disparity in the corresponding area of the world market. A financial crisis that hits a major country sets in motion a damaging ripple effect that is felt worldwide. For example, damage done by the recent financial crises in the United States and euro countries have been enormous within both advanced countries in the West and elsewhere. China, a country with a huge trade surplus, and other East Asian countries are not exempt from downturns of the global economy.[1] The global economy is not likely to recover anytime soon, and every country in the world, large or small and rich or poor, suffers the consequences.

Before proceeding to discuss global economic disparities in detail, it is important to know open economy macroeconomic principles that facilitate systematic understanding of international trade imbalances, the central part of global economic disparities (GEDs), and their consequences (GHEs). Roles of the central bank are the main part of this chapter. National debt in general is a serious issue. Some countries are still paying off debts related to World War I.

3.1 BASIC PRINCIPLES

There are three essential identities to discuss in this chapter. They are:

1. GNP identity
2. Balance of payments
3. Central bank's balance sheet

Virtually all economic variables, endogenous and exogenous, are directly and indirectly related to each other through these three identities. They provide the basis for deriving the analytical approach to various international economic relationships. Before turning our attention to the ongoing global financial crisis in the next chapter, it is important to understand the theoretical relationships relevant to the crisis. This chapter discusses the nature and causes of global financial crisis on the theoretical foundation and the underlying rationale for relevant policies.

1. GNP Identity

The GNP identity yields the net trade deficit (or surplus) in the foreign sector, decomposed into net spending in the public sector and net investment in the private sector:

$$(M - X) \equiv (G - T) + (I - S) \quad (1)$$

where M = imports, X = exports,
   G = government expenditure, T = tax revenue, I = private investment, S = savings.

Note that the trade deficit $(M > X)$ is not independent of the fiscal deficit $(G > T)$, but they do not add up to a nation's total deficit. Also note that a trade deficit (the foreign sector) is *identically* (by definition) equal to (not caused by) the sum of two net spending in the domestic sectors:
   (a) expenditure over revenue in the public sector (the net public-sector spending)
   (b) investment over savings in the private sector (the net private-sector spending).[2]
   It is a simple identity but has important policy implications for global economic crises, including the crises prevailing currently in the United States and euro countries. The above identity implies that a deficit in the foreign sector is financed by the public sector (fiscal deficit) and/or the private sector, and *vice versa*. Larger trade deficits in a country require, *ceteris paribus*, larger fiscal deficits. There was an actual case politicized by this correlation in the 1980s. In the United States, the House bill (H.R.3) for enactment of the Omnibus Trade and Competitiveness Act of 1988 (OTCA) was submitted in 1986, when political turbulence over increasing trade deficits and fiscal deficits was at its peak.[3] If deficits in both foreign and public sectors are excessive beyond permissible levels, the central bank also intervenes to not finance the deficits of these two sectors directly but to boost the private sector. The Fed's quantitative easing (QE) is an example.

2. Balance of Payments (BP)

The BP table is an accounting statement of all economic transactions between residents in a country and residents in the rest of the world recorded systematically in accordance with the double-entry bookkeeping principle. It exhibits the country's status of not only exports and imports of goods and services but also outflows and inflows of short-term and long-term capital and the official reserves. The top half of the table is concerned with the balance of international transactions of goods and services, referred to as the "current account"; the bottom half shows the balance on financial transactions, referred to as the "capital," "financial" or "asset" account. Given the fundamental double-entry accounting identity that the total of the credit side equals the total of the debit side, the current account balance, either surplus or deficit, must be numerically matched by the capital account deficit or surplus, respectively; thus the BP is written as:

$$CA + KA \equiv 0 \text{ (2)}$$

where CA = balance in the current account, KA = balance in the capital account or asset account.[4]

Rearranging components of KA in identity (2) yields a measure for international indebtedness that is equivalent to:

Net home country's international investment position (IIP)
    = Home country's assets abroad (HAA)
    - Foreign country's assets in the home country (FAH), (3)
    where HAA = official reserve assets + other government assets + private assets
    FAH = official assets including reserves + private assets.

There are two ways to explore the causes of global economic disparities or financial crises: imbalance in transactions of goods and services and imbalance in financial transactions. The amount of surplus in the current account is equivalent to the amount of deficit in the capital account. The amount of trade deficits on the current account basis (the real sector) of the balance of payments (BP) in a country is what the country owes to the rest of the world, that is, borrowing from abroad (the monetary sector). The duality here resembles the classical dichotomy in macroeconomics.

    The identity (2) contains important policy implications of the debt in a country that is the country's trade deficits accumulated over time. A debt is what a country owes to another country. It is the country's net borrowing from a foreign country in exchange for its bills and bonds. There is no difference in practices between private and public lending and borrowing. A lender buys bonds issued by a borrower in the case of a private transaction. Equivalently, a lending country obtains bills and bonds issued by the government of a borrowing country in the case of a public transaction. The amount of borrowing from foreign countries is the same as the amount of assets (security, bank deposit, and direct investment) given up to foreigners. The same principle is applicable to intra-country and inter-country financial transactions. In general, a debt represents the degree of financial indebtedness of the country to other countries. The debt-service ratio is an important index used for credit rating of a country. As a serious trade disparity, a chronic trade deficit in a country is the epicenter of a global financial crisis. The magnitude of the disparity determines the scale and intensity of the crisis. Although the dynamic pattern of a global economic crisis is not readily traceable in the real world, the disparity-crisis causality shows the pattern of a crisis moving toward equilibrium over time. It is theoretically possible to confirm whether the pattern is stable or unstable and oscillatory or nonoscillatory.[5] If a crisis in one country interacts with a crisis in another country, the time path gyrated by two forces could be explosive. Trade surplus is the opposite case of trade deficit and has reverse arguments and policy implications to the case of trade deficits. Trade surplus is equivalent to a claim of the country on the rest of the world.

In principle, there is no reason for concern about the debt held by a country. In the case of the United States, for example, the annual debt-payment ratio (= Debt/GDP) is relatively low because the U.S. GDP is huge and the largest in the world.

In conclusion,

(a) The trade disparity is dual-faceted: trade deficits or surplus in the real sector and outflows or inflows of assets in the financial sector.

(b) By definition, debt is the amount of trade deficits cumulated over time. Excessive and chronic trade deficits of a large country may result in a global or regional debt crisis.

3. Central Bank's Balance Sheet (BS)

A condensed version of the central bank's BS is

$$TA \equiv TL \quad (3)$$

where TA = total assets = domestic assets (DA) + foreign assets (FA)
TL = total liability = currency in circulation (CC) + deposits held by commercial banks (DC).

The total liability (TL), referred to as the "monetary base" (MB), is the narrowest definition of money supply controlled directly by the central bank and thus is the primary instrument of monetary policy. Therefore, the supply of money is not independent of the status of BP (balance of payments) via FA (foreign assets). It is important to make sure that foreign assets consist mainly of official international reserves held by the central bank. Specifically, the central bank often conducts a policy of foreign exchange interventions. If the central bank of a particular country buys (or sells) domestic or foreign assets, both TA and TL in its BS increase (or decrease) simultaneously by the same amount. An increase in TL means an increase in money supply. With a sterilized foreign exchange intervention by the central bank, however, it can keep TL constant. In the case of monetary intervention in a financial crisis, the central bank attempts to tame the crisis usually by means of a "sterilization" (or neutralization) policy that keeps the monetary base constant and/or pursues inter-country coordination of monetary policies before the time path protracts. Such a policy is anti-inflationary and operates within the central bank's balance sheet.

Borrowing and lending between domestic and foreign banks (and investment firms), including domestic and foreign central banks, is an important part of the domain of national monetary policy. It often necessitates monetary policy coordination between central banks. In principle, a country can independently conduct its monetary policy under a flexible exchange rate system. This proposition is often referred to as the "currency substitution hypothesis." Under a managed floating exchange, however, the validity of this hypothesis is somewhat questionable.

Table 3.1 shows reserve assets that include foreign currencies, SDRs, and reserve position in IMF and exclude gold holdings. Figure 3.1 exhibits a sharp asymmetry in international reserve positions between Asia and the rest of the world, both the United States and Europe.

Considering (a) the classical dichotomy of the economy broken down into real and monetary sectors, (b) the relationships among BP, FA, and BS, and (c) the relationship between foreign assets and monetary base in the balance sheet, the trade disparity is related to a wide range of macroeconomic variables. For this reason, central banks in all countries are serious about the status of the external sector.

3.2 NATIONAL DEBTS

As discussed in the previous section, both deficits and surpluses are disparities in the external sector. However, only the countries with deficits are concerned about their chronic deficits (i.e., national debts). Many countries are concerned about external debts. Among them, this section discusses primarily the case of the United States as the country that has

Table 3.1.   International Reserves by Area and Country (in billions of SDRs)[a]

	2009	2010[a]	2011
North America			
U.S.	85.5	78.4	98.3
Canada	34.6	37.0	42.8
Europe	192.6	NA	218.4
France	32.5	36.2	39.0
Germany	47.1	40.5	44.3
Italy	32.0	31.0	33.7
Spain	11.9	12.4	12.8
Greece	1.1	0.9	1.0
Portugal	2.0	2.4	2.8
Switzerland	63.8	145.1	183.1
U.K.	35.9	44.4	52.0
Russia	266.5	NA	296.7
Asia and Pacific			
China	1,542.3	1,861.1	2,087.3
Taiwan	222.6	NA	251.6
India	169.8	178.8	177.3
Japan	652.9	689.3	820.3
Korea, S.	172.2	189.3	198.2
Singapore	119.7	146.6	154.7
Australia	24.9	25.1	28.0
South America			
Brazil	151.5	186.4	228.2
Mexico	63.5	78.1	93.9
M. East/N. Africa	591.3	NA	721.7
World Total	5,481.7	NA	6,973.9

[a] U.S. dollars. The exchange rate is 1SDR = $1.502 as of April 2013.
   NA = not available.
   Source: The Council of Economic Advisors, *Economic Report of the President*, 2013, p. 451.

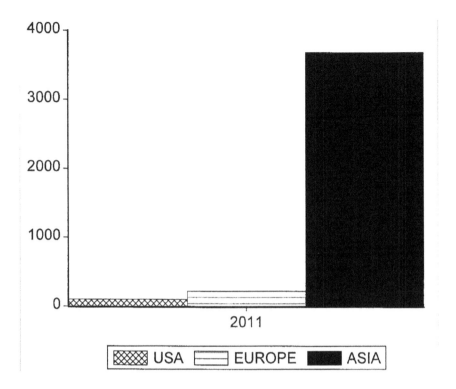

Figure 3.1.   Asymmetry in International Reserve Positions (billions of SDRs).
Note: The exchange rate is SDR 1 = 1.501 as of April 2013. Data: (1) U.S. Census
Bureau, Statistical Abstract of the United States: 2012, Washington, D.C.: U.S.
GPO, p. 872. (2) The Council of Economic Advisors, Economic Report of the
President 2013, Washington, D.C.: U.S. GPO, p. 451.

undergone one of the worst financial crises in its monetary history and
that receives clear counter-repercussions from other major industrial
countries.

Following the bursting of the housing bubble in 2007, the Fed reduced
interest rates to zero in December 2008, maintained the reduced rate over
three years, and continued to maintain the super-expansionary monetary
policy, known as the quantitative easing (QE = expansionary monetary
policy by means of low interest rates and bond purchases from commercial banks), until 2014, the year determined on the basis of optimistic
recovery projections. The QE policy has enabled the United States to
reduce borrowing costs on the amounts of U.S. Treasury bills held by
China. It has kept the dollar depreciated with respect to the yuan as
explained by the asset-market approach to the determination of foreign
exchange rates, thus promoting U.S. exports.[6]

According to the Fed (April 26, 2012), the U.S. economy is making a
recovery, albeit slowly, in the absence of inflationary expectations. Al-

though the liquidity expansion has helped stabilize the financial sector in the absence of inflation, macroeconomic indicators of unemployment, household expenditure, and private investment suggest that the policy has not been successful in boosting the real sector in light of the magnitude of the QE. Amid fears about sustainable growth in connections with the fiscal cliff, inflationary expectations of crude oil and gasoline and, most of all, economic slack in the employment market, the U.S. economy has remained stationary, not sending the Wall Street and foreign financial markets any positive signals toward recovery at present.[7] The estimated total amount released for liquidity expansion by the United States, the European Currency Union (now referred to as "euro zone"), the U.K., and Japan since 2008 is known to be approximately five trillion dollars. This excess liquidity will seriously restrict monetary authorities in conducting monetary policies flexibly in many countries, including emerging countries in the future. Excess liquidity flows in and out of these countries, destabilizing international financial markets and creating a risky environment that adversely affects the real sector in the world economy.

U.S. borrowing since the 1980s has dramatically increased to finance massive fiscal deficits. Lending countries are primarily China, Japan, and other fast-growing Asian economies, including Korea and Taiwan. It is unreasonable to view this type of borrowing as sound. Table 3.2 exhibits U.S. fiscal deficits and trade deficits. Unlike Asian and European countries, the

foreign sector of the United States was small until the 1960s. However, the degree of openness, that is, the volumes of trade (exports and imports in GNP), has steadily increased since 1970s and is now significantly larger. Given recent intercontinental financial crises and the "fiscal cliff" in the United States, mounting trade deficits (i.e., national debt with respect to foreign countries) have become a major concern in economic and geo-economic standpoint.

3.3 DEBT AND STANDING ARGUMENTS

There are a few major standing arguments related to debt:

1. Deficit Complacency

Professor Robert Barro (1975) raised issues about the debt burden, suggesting that the present generation in a country maintains or raises its standard of living by borrowing from future generations, which is equivalent to passing the debt along to future generations.[8] At present, the younger generation is seriously concerned about the future funds for

Table 3.2. Federal Deficits, Gross Federal Debts, Net Interest Payments, and Current Account Balance (in billions of dollars)

	2007	2008	2009	2010	2011
Federal Deficits	-160.7	-458.6	-1,412.7	-1,294.4	-1,299.6
Gross Federal Debt	8,950.7	9,986.1	11,875.9	13,528.8	14,764.2
Net Interest Payment	237.1	252.8	186.9	196.2	230.0
Balance of Current Account	-710.3	-677.1	-381.9	-442.0	-465.9

Source: The Council of Economic Advisors, *Economic Report of the President*, Washington, D.C.: U.S. GPO, 2012, p. 420 and p. 442.

social security and pensions draining down rapidly. It is absolutely necessary for a country of high debt to consume less and save more. Ironically, however, a country cannot afford to be concerned about the future in connection with deficit complacency, even amid fears of country-wide defaults at present. In case of the United States, the standard of living is traditionally rigid. Contrary to a public consensus on austerity needed in the United States, it is difficult to realistically expect savings induced at very low rate of interest and investment during a long stagnation of high unemployment.

2. The Fed's Quantitative Easing (QE) Policy as Deficit Management

The QE policy has been criticized as inflationary. However, it conforms with the economic rationale that a debtor is better off under inflation, whereas a creditor is worse off. It also conforms with the rationale for a depreciation of the dollar with an expansionary monetary policy, as justified by the asset market approach to the determination of foreign exchange rates. A depreciation of the dollar increases U.S. exports. The QE policy is also an attempt to counter inflows of foreign capital, especially from China, into a collapsed housing market after the recent subprime mortgage crisis in the United States.

Apart from the portfolio investment (short-term), there is the practitioner's view suggesting that an abundance of money will always flow from foreign countries into the United States. A considerable amount of U.S. assets held (equivalent to the U.S. trade deficits) by emerging countries with ample low-wage labor and also well-educated labor trained with high technology transferred by multinational corporations, means their greater investment in the United States. Therefore it is necessary to reduce trade deficits in order to reverse this investment and unemployment pattern that is adverse to the United States.

The problem with debt is that it becomes more serious over time due to demographic pressure. Debt divided by population or work force, referred to as the "per capita" debt, clearly suggests that there will be a crisis, *ceteris paribus*, if the population in a country declines and the work force diminishes gradually over time. Given a chain reaction effect among countries in a continent like the EU, the real problem is "as much demographic as financial."[9]

Overall, effects of the financial crisis are multifaceted. It is more urgent to resolve the current crisis than to be solely concerned about the transfer of debts to future generations. The identity and the duality associated with deficit equation 1 above provide the theoretical basis and directions for government policies to reduce deficits over time. These include:

(1) The trade deficits of a country are borrowings from foreign countries. A policy to reduce borrowing from foreign countries is consistent with a policy to reduce trade deficits. This policy calls, in turn, for traditional macroeconomic instruments including foreign exchange and interest rate policies.

(2) Contractionary fiscal policy to achieve a balanced budget is, *ceteris paribus*, consistent with a policy to reduce trade deficits. Fiscal policy is principally the domain of the legislative branch, requiring policy makers to engage in political negotiation for changes in government spending and tax revenue (and currently very difficult and contentious in the United States).

(3) Savings and investment are closely related to monetary policy through monetary instruments, including the rate of interest. A policy to increase savings by means of contractionary monetary policy reduces, *ceteris paribus*, trade deficits.

Note that the trade surplus of a country is the trade deficit of another country. For example, a considerable amount of China's trade surplus is part of the United States' trade deficit. It is often suggested that the current crisis is not a problem of the balance of payments but a problem of borrowing. It is important to keep in mind that a country with trade deficits ultimately becomes a country of borrowing by definition (equations 1 through 3). There are also actual cases in which countries frequently borrow from domestic and foreign sources beyond the level of their trade deficits.

3.4 GEOECONOMIC IMPLICATIONS OF TRADE DISPARITIES

The previous two sections focused on economic principles on external deficits/debts and policy implications. This section examines geoeconomic insights into the background of trade deficits that no country is interested in. In other words, there is no country attempting to trade with other countries in order to build up a negative balance. As a matter of fact, every country realizes that trade surplus increases its economic strength and international political power in a larger share of global markets.[10]

There are geoeconomic implications valid with trade disparity.

(1) Given the chronic surplus and deficit countries, the surplus country boosts its competitive economic power in the world because of the increased amount of foreign assets held by the surplus country. Claims of surplus countries to deficit countries imply shifts of global political power to nations of trade surplus. This has been the case for most of the superpowers.[11]

(2) Trade disputes between two countries, initiated usually by the deficit country, lead to domestic political pressure for bilateral negotiations, efforts to settle the disputes by the WTO, enactment of trade laws, and possibly geopolitical conflicts between them. A country in huge debt with another country is subject to significant political and economic influences by the latter country. At present, China holds a massive amount of short-term U.S. Treasury securities. If China liquidates them, there will be an enormous impact, directly on the U.S. economy and indirectly on global financial markets. The United States needs to regularly assure China that investment in U.S. Treasury securities are safe.

(3) Apart from the above issues related to trade disparities, the (small) volumes of trade, both exports and imports, may cause a policy dilemma in the lack of leverage between trading countries. For example, U.S. exports to and imports from Russia are small, as only 0.7 percent and 0.5 percent of the total, respectively. Western European countries heavily depend on gas supplied by Russia, as high as 32 percent. In connection with the annexation attempt of Ukraine's Crimea in March 2014 by Russia, the United States and EU chose economic sanctions including asset freeze that would accelerate capital flights and the downturn of the Russian economy. In turn, Russia is expanding retaliatory sanctions against West.

NOTES

1. Olivier Blanchard, Director of Research of the IMF, reportedly views that it is difficult to expect recovery until 2018, a decade after the 2008 crisis.

2. It is an identity derived from the GNP identity: Aggregate Supply ≡ Aggregate Demand. Equation (1) is equivalently stated in terms of percentage as: $dz/z = \alpha\,dx/x +$

β dy/y, where z = M-X, x = G-T, y = I-S, α = x/z (x's share or weight in z) and β = y/z (y's share or weight in z), where $\alpha+\beta$ = 1.

3. The OTCA is the first comprehensive trade law since the Smooth-Hawley Tariff Act of 1930 in the United States. See Chung (2006), p. 33.

4. Identities are the standard definitions applied to all countries. The IMF publishes financial statements prepared by member countries in accordance with these definitions in *International Financial Statistics*. In the case of the United States, see *Survey of Current Business* or *Statistical Abstract of the United States*.

5. Dynamic phenomena are mathematically illustrated by means of first- or higher-order single or simultaneous difference or differential equation or equation system.

6. The IMF has recently suggested that China appreciate its yuan (June 2012). This suggestion is reminiscent of controversies on the exchange rate between the dollar and yuan over two decades in the past.

7. It is widely known that Professor Milton Friedman, the Nobel Laureate in Economics in 1976, asserted that "every economic . . . is always and everywhere a monetary phenomenon." Given that the QE policy has been implemented for a sufficient period of time, employment and inflation should have responded to it. It is an intriguing mystery that there is no reaction to the policy so far.

8. Barro, Robert J. (1974), pp. 1095–1117.

9. McArdle, Megan, "Europe's Real Crisis," *Atlantic*, April 2012, pp. 32–35.

10. See Chung (1991), pp. 1–16.

11. Ibid.

FOUR

Financial Crises in the United States

The central part of a global economic disparity (GED) is inter-country imbalances in the foreign sectors. Chronic trade deficits in a country may result in a financial crisis in the country; they may develop to a global crisis (GHE). The duality existing between the current account and capital account in the balance of payments allows us to focus on the financial sector.

Countries are closely related to each other today. The U.S. economy is the main component of the world economy. In the event of a financial crisis in the United States, other countries are seriously concerned about its impact on their economies. This chapter reviews international financial crises in the past and discusses the financial crisis prevailing in the United States. It focuses on policy responses of the Federal Reserve by means of quantitative easing (QE) implemented through three successive phases (November 25, 2008–October 29, 2014).

QE is not a conventional policy. It is highlighted in the appendix at the end of the chapter.

4.1 HISTORY OF FINANCIAL CRISES IN THE WORLD

This section summarizes the history of financial crises over a relatively recent period of time.[1] The stock market crash on October 22, 1929, in the United States, often referred to as "Black Tuesday," is well-known as the biggest crisis in the recent history of the global financial market. Since World War II, economic disparities have emerged among many countries. Trade imbalances, financial crises, and economic recessions have consequently been observed for the past half century. Crises developed in the United States primarily because of its massive trade deficits and realignments of the dollar with respect to other major currencies. There

were also financial crises revolving around LDCs (least developed countries) in the 1980s and 1990s. Chile (1985) negotiated the first debt-of-
equity swaps in an attempt to reduce its debt. Mexico (1994–1995), Brazil
(1999), and Argentina (2001–2002) declined to service their debts and
went into default. At that time, there were U.S. plans like the Baker plan
in 1985 (to maintain net flows of funds for privatization) and the Brady
plan in 1989 (debt reduction subject to economic reform) along with IMF
interventions in an attempt to reschedule debts (deferring payments of
the principal and the interest). In the 1990s, Mexico (1994–1995) and Asia
(1997–1998) experienced large-scale crises. In the case of the Asian financial crisis, it began in Thailand, followed by Malaysia, Indonesia, the
Philippines, and Korea, and also by the Dubai debt crisis afterwards.

Different countries had different reasons for their financial crises. This
book does not discuss them in detail. In general, there was a common
pattern to the crises. The central bank of a country ran out of its dollar
reserves and came under pressure to devalue its currency; it risked possible default and bankruptcy. There were largely three different ways to
resolve the crises:

(a) Rescheduling repayment by bailout lending to banks (i.e., refinancing), as the banks could not afford to write off the debt as a loss

(b) The IMF condition requires a debtor country to meet short-term
loans and long-term reforms involving restrictive fiscal and monetary
policy through higher interest rates, thus to limit foreign exchange depreciation (the asset market approach to foreign exchange determination),
efforts to avoid large budget deficits, and structural reforms of both the
industrial and banking sectors.[2]

(c) All of the crises in the recent past have been serious enough to
warrant holding summit meetings (between governments) and conferences or annual meetings of the IMF-World Bank. The Smithsonian
Agreement (1971) and the Plaza Agreement (1985) are examples. The
Smithsonian Agreement changed the foreign exchange regime from a
fixed to a managed floating exchange system, and the Plaza Agreement
concerned the value of the dollar appreciating with respect to other key
currencies. The arguments associated with each crisis have chiefly been
about chronic trade disparity in a country as the cause, and realignment
of the foreign exchange rate between relevant currencies as the result. At
that time, the trade surplus and currency of Japan (yen) were the primary
issues in the global economy, just as the trade surplus and currency of
China (yuan) are main concerns today.

Traditionally, there has been a common pattern of trade deficits in a
country that has fallen into debt with respect to another country, which
raises questions about debt repayment in the face of a near default; and
large chronic debt mounting over time may lead to a financial crisis. As
observed in the most recent global financial crisis, serious disparities in
world trade have eventually precipitated the various international finan-

cial/economic crises. The financial crisis of the United States occurring in 2008 is the latest crisis since 1929. It has continued for over five years as of today. It appears to be the worst crisis in the post–World War II era. The contagions diffused to euro countries were almost instantaneous and have now resulted in a major economic stagnation around the world, including in the Asian economy. The frequency of crises, large or small, is expected to increase in the future.

This chapter first discusses the general nature and causes of an international financial crisis and then examines specifically the ongoing financial crises in the United States and euro countries and their impact on the Asian economy.

4.2 FINANCIAL MARKETS

A financial market in a country consists of a bond market and a stock market. Logically, the origin of a *domestic* financial crisis is either one of these two markets or both. The same rationale is applicable to international financial crises. There are two different kinds of international investment: long-term (direct) and short-term (portfolio) investment. A *global* financial crisis is a crisis that stems from the domain of portfolio investment.

Table 4.1 presents (1) U.S. owned assets abroad and (2) foreign owned assets in the United States for the period from 2005 to 2010. The difference between (1) and (2) is the U.S. net investment position in each year. It is important to note that the GDP share of the U.S. financial sector has steadily increased since 1940. In the financial sector, the size of the bond market is enormous. Figure 4.1 represents a series of credit market borrowing during the latest period, the period of the first financial crisis in the United States. Note that the borrowing increased dramatically since 2007, until 2010.

There are two different kinds of U.S. Treasury securities: Bills (three month and six month both in auction) and constant maturities, (three year, ten year and thirty year), often called "notes and bonds." Treasury securities are usually inflation adjusted. One can also measure the size in terms of the total traded amount per day, month, or year; the number of domestic and foreign stock markets; and the number of stock price indexes. There are forty-three major stock markets in the world. Major stock market indexes are domestic indexes (New York Stock Exchange indexes, Dow-Jones Industrial Average (DJI), Standard and Poor's Composite Index, and Nasdaq Composite Index) and foreign stock market indexes

Table 4.1.   U.S. International Investment Position (in billions of dollars)

	2005	2006	2007	2008	2009	2010
U.S. Owned Assets Abroad	11,962	14,428	18,400	19,465	18,512	20,298
Foreign Owned Assets In the U.S.	13,894	16,620	20,196	22,725	20,834	22,772
U.S. Treasury Securities	1,341	1,558	1,737	2,401	2,880	3,365

Source: The Council of Economic Advisors, *Economic Report of the President*, Washington, D.C.: U.S. GPO, 2011, p. 447.

(London FTSE 100, Tokyo Nikkei 225, Hong Kong Hang Seng, Germany DAX-30, Paris CAC-40, and Dow Jones Europe STOXX 50).

In addition, U.S. financial investors today are extremely knowledgeable about international financial markets, including markets for financial derivatives, and they are skillful at making transactions of financial assets through the super-speed global Internet network.

In such a keen market, a financial market may easily be out of a normal trajectory, and crisis would occur.

4.3 U.S. FINANCIAL CRISIS

This section discusses the on-going financial crisis and associated policies in the United States.

4.3.1 Background and Economic Situations

The Great Depression of the 1930s is regarded as the worst crisis in the history of the U.S. economy. It was characterized by:

predominant duration of five years (October 22, 1929 through 1933; actually lasted until World War II in a less severe form, including second downturn that occurred around 1937–1937);
stock market collapse (Black Tuesday) from DJI 381 to 230;
decrease in GNP in 1933 by 30 percent; and

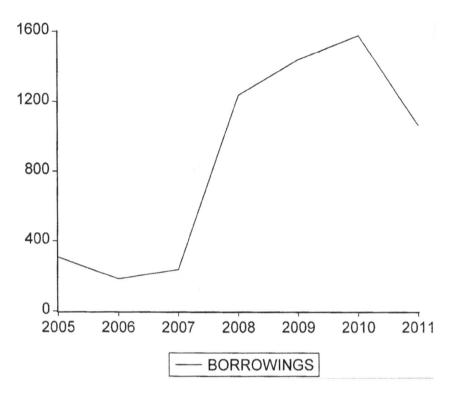

Figure 4.1.   U.S. Credit Market Borrowings (billions of dollars of Treasury Securities). Data: The Council of Economic Advisors, Economic Report of the President, 2012, Washington, D.C.: U.S. GPO, p. 12.

unemployment rate of 25 percent.

Later, there was a period of post–World War II prosperity for over two decades in the United States, followed by a period of long stagnation caused mostly by the two major oil crises in the 1970s. The downturn of today is characterized by:

duration over five years;
stocks at their lowest level in November 2008;
unemployment at one time around 10 percent;
fiscal deficit, defense spending, and trade deficit in disputes;
price of gasoline once above four dollars per gallon.

As the financial market became increasingly tense in turbulence, considerable uncertainty prevailed along with rigid liquidity. Economists began to cautiously warn that global economic imbalances would derail the world economy. In December 2007, the National Bureau of Economic Research (NBER) announced that the U.S. economy was in *recession*.

Concurrently, many economists were concerned about unusual behavior on Wall Street and its potential impact on the economies of the rest of the world. Professor Robert Shiller (2000) suggested that housing prices peaked in 2006 on his *price-earnings ratio* and predicted the bursting of the housing bubble in 2007–2008 and the worldwide recession. Mass media began to cover various views on the overall condition of the world economy at that time:

- A dynamic Asian economy, including the economies of China and India which grew at annual rates of 8.9 percent and 7.7 percent, respectively, before the crisis;
- A sharp increase in income gap between the top 20 high-income group of countries and the bottom 20 low-income group of countries;
- Uncertainty in foreign exchange markets amid the appreciation of China's yuan with respect to the dollar;
- Tight money policies across many countries to cope with inflationary expectations due to higher prices of energy and raw materials,
- Emergence of a new industry to develop alternative energy sources in response to chronic shortages of oil and environmental regulations;
- R&D activities in high technology became globalized to reduce production costs;
- Industries in China and India became increasingly global in scale through M&A (mergences and affiliations);
- A second revolution in super-high-speed Internet systems run by means of infrared and gamma rays that will control communications, mass media, and commercial transactions in the near future;
- Emergence of foreign industries in Japan and Korea that may eventually replace American industries such as automobile manufacturing.

4.3.2 Government Spending

Excess spending by the public sector, the primary cause of national debt, has long been a serious issue worldwide. In the United States, the main concern has naturally been focused on the U.S. public debt that is not independent of its trade deficit. Statistics on trade deficits (e.g., $805 billion in 2005) and borrowing (3 trillion dollars since 1999) delineate the situation of the United States in needing to sell stocks, bonds, and businesses. The cumulative amount of trade deficits for the past twenty years was large enough for the United States to become the biggest debtor in the world. As of September 2012, the amount of U.S. national debt reached 16 trillion dollars at a time when the current debt ceiling was set at 16.39 trillion dollars. This is comparable to the U.S. GDP of 14.2 trillion dollars in 2011. There was no doubt that the government would reach the debt limit before the end of the year (2013) without a dramatic improvement in the foreign sector and that the legislative branch would therefore have to pass a law to raise the debt limit for 2013, most likely subject to a debt-reduction plan imposed on the Obama Administration. At the time of writing this book, the White House and the House of Representatives are facing off at a *fiscal cliff* of tax rates (December 2012–January 2013), followed by the period of the recent government shutdown and debt limit confrontation of October 2013 between the administration and the House.

Table 4.1 shows amounts of U.S. Treasury securities held by domestic and foreign investors in 2011. It is notable that American investors own 69 percent (over two-thirds) of U.S. Treasury securities, whereas foreign investors hold 27 percent. The latter number is much smaller than commonly believed. In a recent issue of *Economic Report of the President,* the Council of Economic Advisors to the President suggests that "foreign investors own only about 11 percent of the overall financial assets in the U.S. economy." China and Japan own only 7 percent (roughly 1.2 trillion dollars) and 6 percent of the total issued by the Treasury, respectively. Although these amounts are significant enough to impact global financial markets, there has been a public misconception about the amount of U.S. Treasury securities held by China and Japan.

In any event, such unilateral borrowing repeated over time is not a healthy way to run an economy. The huge amount of U.S. government borrowing that generated a hemispheric imbalance before 2008 was clearly a precursor to the financial crisis. Nonetheless, there was also a positive side of the borrowing. It probably prevented a collapse in the dollar and enabled the United States to carry out rescue programs during the financial crisis.

It is important to keep in mind that the economic and political status of China and other emerging countries in Asia has recently risen through rapid growth, whereas the status of both the United States and Europe have gradually fallen. This is not to suggest that economic deterioration in the West as a whole is desirable but rather that the centuries-old economic disparities between the East and the West that are likely equilibrated through free competition in the world market are mutually beneficial for the entire world. Although some economists would criticize the fact that these emerging economies in Asia, especially China, are heavily subsidized by the government (i.e., "state capitalism"), it is more desirable for the world as a whole in the long run if the Asian economy emerges rather than remains reclusive.

4.3.3 *Precursors of the Current Crisis*

In its issues of *World Economic Outlook* for the period between 2006 and 2010, the IMF assessed the overall status of the U.S. economy as "uncertainty of housing market—turbulences in financial markets—a long-term stagnation of the world economy.", The world economic situation for the four years before and after the crisis is summarized as follows:

> 2006 Robust growth set to continue but with an uncertain housing market in the United States;
> 2007 A short-term risk and economic slowdown in the United States is recognized and
> spillover across countries noted.
> 2008 Financial turbulence and economic downturns reported. Global growth projected
> to decelerate from 4.9 percent in 2007 to 4.1 percent in 2008.
> 2009 Both short-term and medium-term crisis prospects predicted, and macroeconomic policies to reduce uncertainty and systemic risk in financial
> markets discussed.
> 2010 Recovery amid inflationary pressures in the financial sector expected. World
> economic growth projected at about 4.5 percent in 2010 and 4.25 percent in 2011.

The overall situation of the world economy did not favorably develop for the U.S. economy:

- The United States has continued to accumulate external debts due to massive trade and fiscal deficits since the early 1980s.[3]
- The European economy shows no sign of economic vitality amid concerns about the impact of high oil prices on inflation. Germany and France, the two biggest euro countries, grew at rates close to zero.
- In contrast to the U.S.-EU economies, the Asian economy continued to grow.

Asymmetry in the global economy began to emerge. Foreign assets and foreign reserves that accumulated mostly in U.S. dollar assets exposed the world economy to considerable risk.

World economic "proceedings" before and after the bankruptcy of Lehman Brothers and policy responses to the crisis by the U.S. Treasury and Federal Reserve are compiled below in chronological order. The primary information sources are mass media including the *Wall Street Journal* and *Financial Times*.

Early 2000s Periods of imbalances among economies of the United States, Europe and Asia. Economists began to worry about the asymmetrical development of the world economy.

2005 5/4–5 S&P slashed bond ratings of the two biggest automakers to junk status. Increases in sales of Toyota, Honda, and Nisan in the U.S. market by 21.3 percent, 13.6 percent, and 27 percent, respectively, for the year since 2004.

7/21 China abandoned an 11-year-old peg of the yuan at 8.28 to the dollar and adopted a managed floating exchange rate system linked to a basket of major currencies subject to central parities at the end of each day.

2006 U.S. trade and fiscal deficits continued to increase.

2007 12 *Recession* began in the United States, the longest downturn in a quarter century.

2008 9/15 Lehman Brothers, a financial services firm holding 600 billion dollars in assets,

filed for Chapter-11 bankruptcy protection. Its freewheeling subprime mortgage practices housing-related assets resulted in unprecedented financial loss.

1. Congress approved the Troubled Asset Relief Program (TARP) of 700 billion dollars.

11/20 Stocks and bonds fell to their lowest levels since the outbreak of the economic crisis. The share price of Citigroup fell more than 60 percent. The largest single-month decline of consumer prices in October since World War II raised concerns about deflation in the United States.

11/21 Sharp increases in unemployment rates in the U.S. as employers cut 533,000 jobs in November, the most in 34 years, adding up to 1.9 million jobs lost since the recession began in December 2007. The rate of unemployment rose to 6.7 percent, indicating that the country had tipped into its deepest recession since the first oil crisis in 1974 and was revived again in 1982 under the Reagan administration.

11/25 The U.S. Treasury attempted to rescue Citigroup by injecting 20 billion dollars from the TARP in addition to 25 billion dollars.

The European economy began to show signs of slowdown.

The U.S. government announced another 800 billion dollars for financial expansion, much of it directly from the Fed: 600 billion dollars to purchase debt issued or backed by mortgage firms and 200 billion dollars for consumer loans to students, car buyers, and small businesses. In response to the refinancing for home owners and buyers, mortgage costs fell sharply. However, housing sales did not rebound, because of job and income losses in 2007–2008.

12/2 As the recession continued to drag on longer and deeper, the Fed cut the Federal funds rate (a key short-term interest rate) from 1 percent and was inclined to keep cutting it further to near zero. In an attempt to reduce long-term interest rates that would lower mortgage costs, the Fed bought not only Treasury securities but also corporate bonds and equities. Also private investors switched money, stocks, corporate bonds, and municipal bonds into U.S. Treasury bonds, seen as safe havens in a time of uncertainty. The Dow industrials fell 7.7 percent. The S&P 500 fell 8.9 percent.

12/5 The European Central Bank announced a three-quarter percentage point drop in its main policy interest rate. Chrysler, GM, and Ford asked Congress for 34 billion dollars in emergency aid.

12/16 Bernard L. Madoff, a financier in New York, was accused of masterminding a Ponzi scheme, stealing billions of dollars from pension funds, charities, and other sources he solicited for investment in exchange for annual returns as high as 46 percent. He was found guilty of 11 federal felonies. The money missing from client accounts in his firm was almost 65 billion dollars.

The Federal Reserve slashed the Federal funds rate to 0.25 percent, effectively zero, the lowest in 54 years.

12/17 Saudi Arabia announced the largest cut of OPEC output in order to stop declining prices.

12/19 The Bush administration approved an emergency bailout of the U.S auto industry amounting to 17.4 billion dollars. Ford Motor declined to receive a rescue loan.

2009 3/10 Congress approved this 2009 "stimulus" spending package bill of about 700 billion dollars.

3/12 Bernard Madoff pled guilty to financial fraud. The fallout spread through global financial markets.

5/1 Chrysler filed for Chapter-11 bankruptcy protection.

The recession pronounced formally by the NBER in December 2007 is the landmark of this crisis. There was a significant decline in economic activity spread across the economy, lasting more than a few months, normally visible in production, employment, real income, and other indicators. The rate of inflation was only 2 percent, the rate of unemployment was 9.6 percent (7.3 million people unemployed), the average price of houses dropped by 30 percent, and the population at the poverty level ($21,756 and below for the annual income for a family of four) increased.

The bankruptcy of Lehman Brothers that directly launched the financial crisis in 2008 seriously damaged the U.S. economy. It is also inconceivable that a financial crisis could occur without underlying problems prevailing in short-term capital markets. Problems existed in accountability and transparency of the financial system, the "too-big-to-fail" issue, bailouts, and abusive financial service practices. The executive and legislative branches of the government collaborated to enact the Dodd-Frank Wall Street Reform and Consumer Protection Act in 2010 for financial reform. It is the most important financial law passed since the well-known Glass-Steagall Act of 1933 that prohibited combined investment (proprietary) and commercial banking and whose repeal contributed to the lax banking regulation that helped cause the 2008 crisis.

4.4 POLICY RESPONSES TO THE FINANCIAL CRISIS

Since the Great Depression in the 1930s, the U.S. economy has been experiencing the most difficult time ever due to recession-stagnation under the financial crisis that began in the second half of 2008. Ever since the crisis, the stock market in New York has fluctuated radically. News on drops of all benchmark indexes—the DJI verage, S&P's Index, and Nasdaq Composite Index—became ubiquitous. Decliners outpaced advancers on the New York Stock Exchange. Also, global markets continued to slide alongside the U.S. stock market. It was around this time that China began to think of U.S. Treasury securities as risky assets and decided to liquidate them for two consecutive months before the end of 2010. China might have thought about the burden to the United States if investors sell securities issued by the government, their prices decrease, and the government then offers higher interest rates to attract investors.

The United States has strived for economic recovery by means of a wide range of rescue programs to avoid default. Without them, the United States could have plunged into default. Initially, there was a sharply divided political stalemate on the recovery program, especially regarding the statutory debt limit. On November 26, 2008, the government pledged to provide an additional 800 billion dollars, of which 600 billion dollars was for the Fed to buy the debt issued by mortgage firms and 200 billion dollars was for consumer lending provided by the Fed's quantitative easing. As a result, mortgage rates dropped and refinancing to reduce mortgage costs surged. It was a critical time, to the extent that the administration prioritized payments on the order of interest on U.S. Treasury bonds, Social Security, Medicare and Medicaid, military spending, and other social safety net programs.

There were basically three financial policy measures, outlined below. (For details, see the appendix to this chapter.)

1. Specific Facilities and Programs Provided by the U.S. Treasury

There are various facilities and programs implemented in concert with the Federal Reserve. They were available before and after the financial crisis in 2008; each of them has specific subparts.

2. The Budget Control Act of 2011 (Pub.L. 112–25)

Congress passed the Budget Control Act of 2011 on August 2, 2011, which has served as the federal budget for fiscal year 2013 (October 2012–September 2013). This act increased the debt ceiling and mandated reduced governmental spending without tax increases.

The Budget Control Act of 2011 produced a downgraded U.S. credit rating by S&P from AAA to AA⁺ the first ever in U.S. history on August 5, 2011. The downgrade reflected the fact that the U.S. government did not exert enough effort to reduce its huge debt. The S&P's decision would increase U.S. borrowing costs of government bonds and eventually of consumer loans for autos, mortgages, and corporate debts. The table below, which is based on the *Washington Post*, (August 11, 2011, p. 1) shows how Wall Street immediately reacted to the S&P's downgrading.

The Dow Jones Index, (average of 500)

Monday, August 8	Down 635 points (- 5.6 percent)
Tuesday, August 9	Up 430 points (+4.0 percent)
Wednesday, August 10	Down 520 points (-4.6 percent)

The turmoil in the U.S. stock market immediately led to radical fluctuations in stock markets around the world and heightened concerns about global recession.

3. Quantitative Easing (QE) by the Federal Reserve Board

In response to defaults and foreclosures in the housing market, widespread bankruptcies of banks and financial firms, and a rate of unemployment in 2008 that remained as high as 8 percent in the first years of the economic crisis (2008–2010), the Fed's policy was a series of monetary expansion measures. The objective was to keep long-term interest rates at or close to zero through open-market purchases of longer-maturity Treasury securities held by commercial banks and also mortgage-backed securities. Money generated through three phases of the QE policy during the period of Ben Bernanke's tenure as chairman of the Federal Reserve was to be put back into the economic system.[4]

Given uncertainty about the future of the U.S. economy and the limited capacity of the executive branch to maneuver fiscal policy because of the political deadlock with the legislative branch, the Fed's QE policy safeguarded the U.S. economy from a panic. This approach is based on Milton Friedman's philosophy of *"money matters,"* implying that every economic issue or problem is basically a monetary phenomenon. Monetarists, including the Fed's chairman Ben Bernanke, after eight decades from the Great Depression on, who are faithful to the argument in the work done by Friedman and Schwartz (1963), did not want to repeat the Fed's "passive, defensive, and hesitant" policy that allowed the great contraction.

It is solely attributable to the Fed's consistently maintained QE policy that the enormous household debt accrued from home mortgages and credit cards decreased by 11 percent in July 2012, equivalent to 600 billion dollars, in comparison with 2007.

In addition, the global financial crisis resulted in a sudden halt in capital flows to countries other than the United States, enabling the United States to borrow at low interest rates abroad.[5] Ironically, the United

States has become a big borrower. The reduced borrowing costs made it possible for the Fed to "involve deploying operations for purchases of credit and assets financed by increasing reserves—the mirror image of the quantitative easing," including purchases of securities issued by mortgage finance businesses with close ties to the government (Fannie Mae, Freddie Mac, Ginnie Mae, Federal Home Loan Banks) and purchases of U.S. Treasury bonds. The size of the Fed's balance sheet continued to expand, and excess reserves of commercial banks increased to counter credit contraction, reflecting the banks' disinterest in lending money.[6,7] The Fed was able to stabilize the U.S. economy during a dangerous time period. However, there is little clear indication of significant increase in employment or growth despite successive applications of QEs over a long enough time period until 2014. In the absence of any magical tools for the Fed except QE policy during Bernanke's tenure, however, an enormous amount of inflationary "magma" has dangerously been built up by this policy. In testimony before the Senate Banking Committee on July 17, 2012, Federal Reserve Chairman Bernanke admitted that the U.S. recovery had lost momentum in recent months and that a dark outlook was ahead; he appealed to Congress to take action to avoid a fiscal cliff.

4.4.1 Macroeconomic Perspectives

The current monetary economic situation of the United States corresponds to the flat segment of the Keynesian LM curve (a graphical representation of the monetary sector in the graphical space of income-rate of interest) at a near-zero rate of interest. The Fed's supply of money on the Friedman-Bernanke line at present merely extends the LM curve out to the right. Given the so-called liquidity trap and the IS curve (a graphical representation of the real sector) which is stationary, any attempt to recover the U.S. economy solely by the QE policy is therefore not fruitful. Presumably for this reason, Bernanke urges Congress to avert a fiscal cliff on taxes and spending. Even at a near-zero rate of interest, the IS curve is not moving to the right at present in the absence of an expansionary fiscal policy. It is now Congress's turn to move the IS curve to the right for sustainable growth. In the absence of Congressional action, the U.S. economy stubbornly remains in a quagmire no matter which direction a policy maker would spin the policy handle.

Several additional comments are as follows:

- Monetary expansion under the QE policy should have depreciated the dollar and promoted U.S. exports, in accordance with the monetary and asset approaches to determination of foreign exchange rates. No significant effect, however, has taken place so far in the foreign sector. The Fed has clearly reached the limit of its capacity in dealing with post-crisis economic problems not only at home but abroad as well.

- Given serious uncertainty in domestic and international economies, investors are only in favor of safe assets, such as U.S. Treasury bonds or idle cash held in banks, including Swiss banks, instead of stocks. According to the theory of portfolio selection, the risk premium is supposed to be exceedingly high at present. However, risk averters do not care about it. Their hedging behavior for safe assets may slow down worldwide stock markets and extensively aggravate the international economy. Recession prevailing in the global economy at present discourages international trade and investment and reduces asset values. During such a risky period, it is important to employ a credible policy to reduce uncertainty for household consumption and business investment.

- At present, sluggish world economies are feeding on each other. The U.S. economy has remained in a slump for too long with a still high rate of unemployment (7.7 percent as of March 2013), only a little reduced from a range of 8–8.2 percent during the peak of the crisis.[8] Counting "discouraged workers," the effective total rate of unemployment would be even higher. Amid high prices of gasoline and food, there has been no significant increase in exports of U.S. goods and services. The financial crisis in Europe and a slower performance in the Asian economies, including those of China and Japan, are the primary cause. Such a worldwide stagnation necessitates policy coordination among the United States, the EU, and Asia.

- The real rate of interest is what investors care about. In terms of Fisher's identity ($r = i/p^e$, where r = real rate of interest, i = nominal rate of interest, and p^e = inflationary expectation), inflationary expectation is not known under high uncertainty, and the real rate of interest cannot be calculated. Investors have thus lost a proper guide for their investment. In addition, the nominal rate of interest is close to zero in the United States and is less than 1 percent in the EU.

4.4.2 U.S. Economy Today

The United States is the largest debtor in the world today. During 2012, which included a presidential election, bipartisan politics deadlocked on congressional spending control amid existing debt and trade deficits. This resulted in a sudden decrease in fiscal spending with no tax increases, known as the *fiscal cliff*. The Congressional Budget Office predicted that the U.S. economy will again fall in a deep recession with a big increase in tax revenue and a spending cut amid dissonance between the legislative and executive branches.[9]

Specific issues are:

(1) The Republican Party pushed for a policy to extend all of the Bush tax cuts, which reduces tax revenue by one trillion dollars, whereas the Democratic Party asserted that a heavy tax be imposed on wealthy people.
(2) The upper-middle-income class needs to pay the alternative minimum tax for the next year.
(3) The 2 percent Social Security payroll tax cutis terminated by the end of 2013.

The White House wants to raise the income tax rate from 35 percent to 39.6 percent for those earning above 250,000 dollars per year, whereas the House pursues a very different agenda—cut domestic social spending, reduce tax deductions, and prevent tax evasion in order to achieve a balanced budget. The American economy has experienced even a *sequester* (defined as proportional spending cuts across all federal agencies) beginning in March 2013. Amid the political deadlock in Congress, the executive branch does not have an effective fiscal instrument to deal with the economic crisis. Fortunately, however, reconciliation finally occurred, in a limited way with the FY 2014–2015 budget deal of December 2013. Despite serious efforts to achieve economic recovery from the debt crisis, there has been no tangible result in employment or economic growth suggesting that the U.S. economy significantly responds to policy measures. The U.S. economy speeded up late in 2013 along with a faster drop in the unemployment rate to 7 percent only for a brief period, but it is not still on a healthy track.

A historic experiment of the QE policy stirred comments about its effects in the market, including those by professors Edmund Phelps, Paul Krugman, Michael Spence, and Allan Meltzer through mass media and conferences during the peak time of QE policy (*Wall Street Journal*, *New York Times*, www.ft.com, and *Atlantic*'s Economy Summit, respectively). Phelps warned of uncertainty associated with the fundamentals under which higher interest rates and unemployment may prevail in the near future; Krugman, pointed out that prevention of depression only by means of increasing liquidity is not easy; Spence asserted governments and central banks to break the downward spiral of asset prices and economic activity; Meltzer was critical about QE on the grounds that the Fed was acting outside of its traditional lending facility to make loans to commercial banks. At present, studies conducted rigorously for publications in journals and books are limited. Congleton (2009) suggests the political response by standing institutions at crisis management relative to innovative legislation. In his book, Rickards (2011) criticized the QE policy as the policy transferring the risk of the United States to the rest of the world. The policy is globally inflationary, changes foreign exchange rates, and increases high interest rates as a result of a tight monetary policy in the United States.

As Bernanke's term ended by January 31, 2014, it was expected that the Fed was tapering off QE. In June 2013, the Fed announced that its QE policy would gradually be phased out over the next three years in three stages: slowdown, suspension, and absorption. The Fed under new chair Janet Yellen has inclined toward terminating the QE framework. After the sharp contraction since the recession ended, the U.S. economy has sent signals of rebounding. In June 2014, the Fed announced that the Federal Open Market Committee (FOMC) would terminate the quantitative easing (of 3.630 trillion dollars to purchase bonds through three consecutive QE phases implemented for about six years since 2008) at the upcoming October meeting, subject to the current recovery of U.S. economy continuing. On October 29, the Fed finally ended QE (of 4.480 trillion dollars) on its positive assessments of unemployment and inflation.

The Fed accomplished its main goal of reducing unemployment. However, it is expected that interest rates in the United States will eventually be higher, and the U.S. economy will be sluggish in the long run. Despite a stronger dollar in the future, forecasts on exports from foreign countries to the United States may not necessarily be optimistic.

APPENDIX: QUANTITATIVE EASING

A central argument of macroeconomics in the 1960s and 1970s concerned the choice of policy to deal with inflation and unemployment, two fundamental economic problems, and their trade-off (often referred to as the "Phillips curve"). Apart from detailed macroeconomic arguments such as the short-run and long-run Phillips curves, Keynesians believed in the effectiveness of fiscal policy, whereas monetarists believed in the effectiveness of monetary policy. Professor Friedman, the Nobel Laureate in Economics in 1976, contended that every economic issue or problem is a monetary phenomenon in the long run.

Some economists attribute the causes of the Great Depression to the real sector, such as lack of investment and government spending to balance the budget, whereas others attribute the causes to the monetary sector, such as a tight money policy in response to the speculative bubble in the stock market. In particular, Friedman and Schwartz (1963) criticized "the Fed's passive, defensive and hesitant policy allowing a large decrease in the nominal supply of money that caused the great contraction." Bernanke (1983) asserted that the series of bank closings helped to start and aggravate the Great Depression. At a conference on Friedman's ninetieth birthday in November 2002, Ben Bernanke, then a governor of the Fed, regretted the Fed's disregard of Friedman's proposition, which predicted that the Federal Reserve could have prevented the Great Depression simply by providing banks with more liquidity.

As asset prices fell, mortgage defaults, foreclosures, and bankruptcies became widespread, and the rate of unemployment remained above 8 percent in 2007 (beginning of the financial crisis of 2008). The Federal Reserve, as lender of last resort to the banking system, determined that the best course of action would be to inject a massive amount of money into the financial system. The objective of this quantitative easing policy is to keep longer-term interest rates at or close to zero by making open-market purchases of both long maturity U.S. Treasury securities held by commercial banks and of mortgage-backed securities, many of which were subprime having almost no real value during the crisis; the generated money is then put back into the economy. The rationale for the Fed policy under Bernanke's leaderships is based on the Friedman-Schwarz argument. In order to cope with the financial crisis of 2008 and its continuing fallout, Chairman Bernanke and his colleagues have been faithfully executing Friedman's proposition. The Fed's expansionary monetary policy is known as *quantitative easing*, denoted QE hereafter. QE has been extended twice, QE2 and QE3, respectively. Dollar bills splashed from Friedman's Helicopter Ben in the *Financial Times* shows what the QE is all about in an esoteric way. Traditionally, the Fed is secretive and opaque to the public. However, by recently making its new strategy to fix the economy transparent, the Fed has made QE credible. This strategy is largely consistent with the theory of rational expectations expounded by Robert Lucas Jr. and Thomas J. Sargent (Nobel Laureates in Economics in 1995 and 2011, respectively).

In September 2011, the Fed performed *operation twist*, a program for stimulating the U.S. economy by selling short-term bonds and simultaneously buying long-term bonds in order to raise prices of long-term bonds and to reduce yields until June 2012. Such a policy was followed by another round from July 2012 to December 2012. The underlying idea of operation twist was to make loans less expensive for those who were interested in buying homes and automobiles by bringing down long-term interest rates. The Fed terminated operation twist ("twist" in terms of yield curve) in December 2012.

We now examine QE by phase. The period of three phases from 2009 to 2012 is a critical test period for the policy actions taken by the Federal Open Market Committee (FOMC).

1. First Phase (QE1): November 25, 2008–1st quarter in 2010

The financial crisis erupted in 2008. The objective of the Federal Reserve was to keep interest rates low by ensuring sufficient liquidity for financial markets through buying up mortgage-backed securities. Such a policy was incorporated with lending facilities: TAF (Term Auction Facility) and TSLF (Term Securities Lending Facility). It is notable that the Federal Reserve originally provided a twenty-eight-day loan to JP Morgan Chase in an attempt to save Bear Stearns investment bank but ultimately approved takeover as bankruptcy became imminent. The Fed also provided a series of credits to banks, small businesses, and consumers; this lowered short-term interest rates successively over time to a near-zero level. Specifically, the Fed provided 100 billion dollars and 200 billion dollars for the two different lending facilities, respectively, in November 2008 and 300 billion dollars in March 2009; and the federal fund rate was reduced from 1 percent to 0–0.25 percent in December 2008. During the period of the first phase, the Fed released 1.7 trillion dollars to purchase Treasury long-term bonds and mortgage securities.

The Fed then required banks to take an annual *stress test* (a test that measures a firm's ability to continue lending during a severe economic downturn) to ensure a minimal level of solvency; this was part of the Fed's financial market infrastructure oversight function (Supervisory Capital Assessment Program). Specifically, it is a short-term scenario test of whether banks have sufficient capital to continue lending in a sudden liquidity crash (analogous to a software crash due to insufficient memory or disk space, etc.). Technically, it is a test on the ratio of net available equity to the total assets of a bank. As of May 2009, there were (a) nine U.S. banks with adequate capital: JPMorgan Chase, Goldman Sachs, Metlife, Bank of New York Mellon, Capital One, American Express, US Bankcorp, State Street, and BB&T; and (b) ten banks needing extra capital: Citigroup, Bank of America, Wells Fargo, GMAC, Morgan Stanley, PNC Financial Services, Regions Financial, Sun Trust, Fifth Third Bankcorp, and Keycorp. Such a test has now become widespread by the FSA in the UK, the European Banking Authority, and the IMF. After three years, fifteen of the nineteen largest banks passed the Fed's latest test. In other words, they had enough capital to withstand a severe recession.[10]

2. Second Phase (QE2): November 3, 2010–June 30, 2011

Since 2010, the Fed has kept the rate of interest low while continuing to purchase long-term Treasury bonds and mortgage-backed securities to cope with the threat of deflation. This policy enabled banks to hold 1.5 trillion dollars for their excess reserves unused and purchase another 600 billion dollars of long-term T-bonds until June 2011, tripling the size of the Fed's balance sheet to 2.9 trillion dollars.

This policy has been heavily debated in political and academic circles. The supporting view states that the policy was to revive a U.S. economy in a severe slump and thus avoid economic panic. The opposing view suggests that the policy is inflationary and flammable if there is no sustainable growth of the economy within a few years. The Fed continued the *operation twist* policy for six months as of June 20, 2012. It planned to sell 267 billion dollars worth of short-term Treasury bonds and buy long-term bonds. In addition, the Fed planned to maintain the federal fund rate at near zero until 2014.

On June 25, 2010, Congress finalized a bank bill to help prevent a crisis in the future. It would create a warning system for financial risks, establish a consumer financial protection bureau that supervises lending practice, force large failing firms to liquidate, and set new rules for unregulated financial instruments.

3. Third phase (QE3): September 13, 2012–October 29, 2014

The Fed announced bond purchases targeting the mortgage market. Included are a purchase of forty billion dollars in bonds per month through the rest of the year in September 2012, followed by an additional forty-five billion dollars, adding up to eighty-five billion dollars a month indefinitely until the economy does not need the support in December 2012, and ultra-low interest rates within a range of 0–0.25 percent extended into mid-2015 to induce investment. The Fed has remained steadfast in its determination to support the economy until the high rate of unemployment (8.1 percent reduced by 0.2 percent) is under control (by means of additional asset purchases and other policy tools). Of course, the Fed is aware that the QE policy is subject to price instability, targeted at a 2 percent expected rate of inflation. This caveat is intended to avoid the lost decade that Japan experienced after its financial crisis. Moreover, the Fed remains cautious about the risk of possible reverse contagion from the euro zone crisis.

It is important to keep in mind that QE was not the only U.S. policy tool to manage the financial crisis. There were/are facilities and programs provided by the U.S. Treasury before and after 2008. The facilities available before the crisis are:

- Asset-backed Commercial Paper Money Market Mutual Fund and Liquidity Facility
- Temporary Guarantee Program for Money Market Funds

The facilities available after the financial crisis include:

- FDIC Guarantee
- Temporary Liquidity Guarantee Program
- Troubled Asset Relief Program (TARP)
- Commercial Paper Funding Facility
- Money Market Investor Funding Facility
- Term Asset–backed Securities Loan Facility
- Government Sponsored Entities Purchase Program
- Government Purchases of Mortgage-backed Securities by Freddie Mac and Fannie Mae

- There were also Congressional actions in an attempt to balance the budget through the Budget Control Act of 2011 (Pub. L. 112–25), featured by an increase in the debt ceiling to match deficit reduction, including the *sequester* in early 2013.

NOTES

1. See Giddy (1994, pp. 297–314) and Melvin (2004, pp. 237–41) on the history of international financial crises.
2. See Krugman and Obstfeld (2003, pp. 324–51) on the asset market approach to the determination of foreign exchange rates.
3. See Chung (2006), p. 33.
4. See the appendix to this chapter for quantitative easing in detail.
5. Euro area (0.75 percent) and Japan (almost zero).
6. See Guha, Krishna, "Fed Dips into Toolbox to Fix Borrowing Costs," *Financial Times*, December 17, 2007, p. 3. In an article contributed to the *Wall Street Journal*, November 24, 2008, p. A19, Wood asserts that an estimated four trillion dollars in housing wealth and nine trillion dollars in stock market wealth was destroyed in the United States.
7. Pre-crisis asset total of the Fed, August 2, 2007, was 874.1 billion dollars, of which the proportion of U.S. Treasury securities was 90.5 percent and the proportion for the other assets was 9.5 percent. Pre-Lehman asset total of the Fed, September 4, 2008 was 905.7 billion dollars; they are 53 percent and 47 percent. Post-Lehman asset total of the Fed, December 11, 2008 was 2,219.1 billion dollars; they are 21.5 percent and 78.5 percent.
8. The rates of unemployment are consistent with those estimated by the OECD.
9. See *New York Times*, May 2, 2012.
10. See *Financial Times*, May 8, 2009, p. 11.

FIVE

Impact of the U.S. Financial Crisis on Economies of Euro Countries and East Asia

Historically, Europe and the United States have been inseparable. They share many common interests and values. Although they have often been in conflicts of economic interest, especially in the realms of trade and finance, their transatlantic economic relationships are traditionally close and cooperative.[1,2] Table 5.1 exhibits U.S. bilateral trade of goods and services and foreign direct investment with euro countries and Asia and Pacific areas. It clearly shows how the intersection between the two economies is broad and deep.

There are basically two different economic institutions in Europe: the European Union (EU with 12 members) and the European Monetary Union (EMU with 15 members) that is represented by the European Central Bank (ECB) of the euro countries. The member countries are not mutually exclusive. Recent financial crises in the euro countries are their contagions of the U.S. crises. The entire process to the contagions is similar to the physical phenomenon of vibrations generated from interactions between a mass (the magnitude of disequilibrium in a country) and another mass (the magnitude of disequilibrium in another country), where the amplitude dampens over time in the process of adjustments toward the new equilibrium through an oscillatory time path.[3] If its financial structure in Europe were strong enough to reject the unhealthy relationship involving bad subprime assets between certain big U.S. and European banks in the first place, the euro zone economy would not have been

Table 5.1. U.S. Trade with Euro Countries and Asia (in billions of dollars, 2009 and 2011)

	X	M	FDI[a]
Euro Countries			
2009	164.9	213.9	1.100.1
2011	198.3	289.3	1,264.7[c]
Asia and Pacific[b]			
2009	291.6	603.7	288.2
2011	418.1	818.9	362.0[d]
Total, all countries			
2009	1,069.7	1,575.1	2,114.5
2011	1,497.4	2,235.8	2,342.8[e]

Notes:

X = U.S. exports to Euro countries and Asia.

M = U.S. imports from Euro countries and Asia.

FDI = Foreign direct investment in the United States.

a. U.S. direct investment in foreign countries in 2008 was 1,1671.6 billion dollars; amounts by area/country are unavailable.

b. X and M for Australia are unavailable.

c., d., e., Amounts in 2010.

Sources:

1. The Council of Economic Advisors, *Economic Report of the President*: 2013.

2. U.S. Census Bureau, *Statistical Abstract of the United States*: 2012, p. 797.

"contagious." Whether or not contagious, the financial crisis in Europe (GHE) is the consequence that reflects poor financial structure (GED).

As many euro countries are sliding into long-term economic lethargy in connection with their financial crises, the EU (not just the EMU) has recently become the target politicized by rightwing politicians in Europe who are skeptical about its existence. They think that the EU cares little about an individual country and has to be replaced (not reformed) by a Europe of free and sovereign nations. The EU is fragile because of the financial crises in EMU countries.

5.1 FINANCIAL RELATIONSHIPS BETWEEN EUROPE AND THE UNITED STATES

The world economy of today is much more open than that of the 1930s. Given the large volume of bilateral trade, both exports and imports, and financial transactions among the United States and euro countries, crises in the euro countries in response to a major financial crisis in the United States are naturally expected. Disequilibrium and displacement in one country creates an equal but opposing force on the economy of another country. The American financial crisis of 2008 was propagated almost instantaneously to Europe; its impact was powerful.

Table 5.2 exhibits U.S. Treasury securities held by domestic and foreign investors. Contrary to the common notion, a dominant proportion held by the United States suggests that the financial crisis was the domestic phenomenon of the United States. Foreign direct investment (FDI) of euro countries to the United States (table 5.1) and U.S. Treasury securities held by European investors verify the close relationships between the two economies. The major financial centers of the world are largely in the EU and the United States. The amount of U.S. securities held by foreign investors, especially China and Japan, is not exceedingly large. The financial crisis in the euro zone was not independent of the crisis in the United States. Although the impact of the U.S. financial crisis on East Asian countries was not as serious as on the EU, countries in East Asia were not independent of the U.S. crisis.

The financial crisis in the United States and its impact on economies of euro countries and East Asia are not over yet. Sections 5.2 and 5.3 discuss the status and ongoing effects in detail by country selected from each area. Since the data required to analyze the situation in the face of individual countries are vast and specific and are not published in a timely fashion by domestic institutions and international organizations as needed, it was often necessary to rely on data available in the mass media only for selected countries.

5.2 CONTAGIONS OF EURO ZONE ECONOMY FROM THE U.S. FINANCIAL CRISIS

The volume of financial transactions through stock exchanges between the two continents is enormous. The impact of the 2008 financial crisis in the United States on the Euro zone was instantaneous and strong. Also, turmoil in Euro countries has now become a problem for the recovery of the U.S. economy. Spiral movements of this turbulence reiterate, and the resulting centripetal force gyrates the world economy in the semblance of an astrophysical "black hole." No single economy can defy the gravity of

Table 5.2.   U.S. Treasury Securities Held by Foreign and Domestic Investors

Foreign investors own roughly one-third of U.S. Treasury securities broken down into:		
	Japan	6 percent
	EU	5 percent
	Other foreign countries	0 percent
	Sub-total	27 percent
Domestic investors and financial centers own two-thirds, broken down into:		
	United States	35 percent
	Intra-U.S. Government	34 percent
	Sub-total	69 percent
Financial Centers		4 percent
Total		100 percent

Source: The Council of Economic Advisors, *Economic Report of the President*, 2011, p. 93.

such a global crisis without strong multilateral policy coordination to prevent the total economic collapse.

During the period of recession in 2008, the rate of unemployment in the Euro zone was 7 percent, (and the annual rate of inflation, 3.2 percent). Professor John Muellbauer asserted that "the world economy is suffering from a Keynesian shortage of demand and it is trapped in a dangerous downward spiral of falling asset prices, rising bankruptcies, foreclosures and unemployment feeding into more of the same, along with falling commodity and now goods prices." He suggested that the world's central banks should jointly buy assets through international coordination, but fiscal policy, though helpful, would not be timely.[4] Monetary policy makes a great contribution to stabilize the U.S. economy in turbulence at present. However, its effect on the real sector, such as growth and unemployment, would be limited in the absence of discretionary fiscal policy in the long run. Given the massive debt, it was and still is impossible to expect reconciliations between the executive branch and legislative branch for additional spending.

This section examines the financial crisis in Euro countries. Table 5.3 shows the main economic indicators of selected countries. Note that there are sharp contrasts between

Germany and the rest of Euro countries, especially Greece as of 2009. Also, debt in the euro zone was already very high in 2009. In Greece, both trade deficits and fiscal deficits were enormous. Greece, Portugal, Spain, and Ireland were on the verge of default. The labor market in Germany was relatively flat, but the rate of unemployment in the euro zone increased from about 10 percent in 2009 to 11.7 percent in December 2012. For the same period, the rate of unemployment in the United States decreased from 10 percent in 2009 to 7.9 percent in in December 2012. As of January 2012, both Spain and Greece are in recession with a highest unemployment rate of 25 percent (*Washington Post*, January 21, 2012, p. A9). Overall, such a euro zone crisis has dragged on for over three years.

What happened in detail? Since 1999, when the *euro*, the common currency in the seventeen Euro countries was created, member countries have been allowed to borrow at the unified rate of interest and did in fact borrow heavily. Bonds issued by southern European member countries were initially considered safe assets to investors. Money flowed subsequently into Greece, but it was revealed that the fiscal deficit figure in Greece had been manipulated. Amid a burst in housing bubbles in the

Table 5.3. Economic Indicators of Selected Euro Countries (2009)

	Greece	Spain	Italy	Germany
(1) GDP Growth (percent)	-3.3	-3.7	-5.5	-5.1
(2) Unemployment Rate (percent)	9.5	18.0	7.8	7.8
(3) Current Account Balance (percent) of GDP)	-11.2	-4.8	-2.0	5.9
(4) General Government Debt (percent of GDP)	128.9	53.9	116.0	74.7

Source: The Council of Economic Advisors, *Economic Report of the President*, 2013, p. 213.

United States and Europe in late 2007, investors began to worry about the possible default of Greece and about struggling economies in Portugal and Spain. They began to withdraw their investments from Greece (and demanded punitive interest rates on its debt). French banks were the most vulnerable to Greek exposure. Italy, Greece, Belgium, and Luxembourg were among the countries in favor of creating euro bonds, whereas Germany was against such creation. Meanwhile, huge losses by Irish banks from housing bubbles resulted in the bailout of Ireland, six months after Greece, on its 370 billion euro debts, followed by Portugal in May 2011.

The crisis in the euro zone during 2011–2012 was almost as serious as the debacle experienced by the United States during 2008–2009, namely the subprime mortgage crisis resulting in the Lehman Brothers bankruptcy and an S&P downgrade of the U.S. credit rating to B+. As the pivotal country in the euro zone, Germany was a financial power house. However, Germany was reluctant and appeared to lose the strength to resolve the debt crisis on its own; its manufacturing sector showed signs of impasse (*New York Times*, May 24, 2012). It was a critical time when investors considered European assets as the assets of high risks without high returns and began to sell off Spanish and Italian bonds.

The European crisis became more complicated. The financial crisis in Greece (May 2012) raised grave concerns about not only the impact on its economy but also on the European Monetary Union and the world economy. Multilateral policy coordination was badly needed. While considering austerity versus growth in Greece, the G-8 meetings held at Camp David in the United States. (May 18–19, 2012) agreed to help Greece stay in the EMU and to promote growth in Europe. After the Camp David meetings, the European debt crisis was still highly volatile. It remains to be seen how this crisis will unfold in the future.

The recent course of European crisis was as follows:

- The European Central Bank (ECB) issued about 600 billion dollars a day, available to member countries for as low as a 1 percent interest rate, on December 21, 2011. Mr. Mario Draghi, the head of the ECB, suggested that he might do the same again, possibly on a larger scale, as needed in the future. Such a policy is similar to the quantitative easing (QE) of the Fed. Despite a rescue fund of about $500 billion cosponsored with the IMF, Europe is still economically fragile.[5]
- The situation of near default was tentatively prevented by the emergency rescue funds provided by the EU and IMF in February 2012.[6] However, the situation was subject to a restrictive fiscal policy for austerity in Greece, including a reduction of employees in the public sector. The backlash in Greece against the austerity program imposed by the EU and IMF resulted in the political failure of a

coalition government, followed by a reemergence of the panicky crisis and a dilemma of choice between the euro and Greek drachma.

- Massive withdrawals of bank deposits raised fears about the spread to other EU countries, a flight of euro assets to Germany, and the demise of the euro zone itself.
- Asset management by hedgers from the risky euro to the relatively safe dollar resulted in the appreciation of the dollar with respect to most key currencies, including the euro, in foreign exchange markets.
- Several other euro zone countries that cannot keep their debt under control and banking system solvent may suffer the same fate as Greece. They are Ireland, Portugal, Spain, and Italy. The Netherlands and the manufacturing sector of the U.K. (a non–euro zone country) were also on this endangered list as of March 2012.
- Given the limited reserves of Greece in the absence of an austerity program, a potential breakup of Greece was possible.
- Euro countries, including Germany, the chief creditor in the euro zone in favor of austerity and tight control by the IMF, prepared to contain the fallout from the Greek disaster and to brace for a possible orderly exit of Greece from the euro bloc.

Germany was criticized because its austerity measures, imposed for years on struggling economies, had contributed to the current European situation. German voters asked why their money should be used for foreigners. The ECB was criticized because emergency rescue funds should be used only the troubled banks. Also, it refused to cut interest rates at a time when countries in trouble could recover through flexible combinations of fiscal austerity and economy-wide monetary expansions (like the Fed intervention [700 billion dollars] in the U.S. economy). In response to sequential crises, Europe is now looking for a system like economic federalism that is managed under tight supervision. Such an institutional approach to control mainly the banking sector in Europe is contrasted with the market-oriented approach to economy-wide recovery in the United States. This seems to be a traditional intercontinental difference in choice of policies. The current situation in Europe requires aggressive macroeconomic policies with international coordination of asset management before a recession threatens to start.

High unemployment in the absence of significant inflationary expectations allows Europe at present to aggressively employ an expansionary monetary policy, that is, lower interest rates. On September 6, 2012, Mario Draghi, president of the European Central Bank (ECB), announced a program to indefinitely purchase euro zone government securities of one- to three-year maturity periods in order to reduce the borrowing cost and expected rate of inflation. The rationale for this policy is similar to that of the operation twist employed by the U.S. Federal Reserve in 2011–2012.

The effects of financial crises in the United States on economies of euro and East Asian countries are not over yet. The next two sections summarize by country what their situations are and how they have unfolded so far through the periods of crises in the two continents, respectively.

5.3 FINANCIAL CRISIS IN THE EURO AREA BY COUNTRY

This section examines briefly the cases of three selected countries.

1. Italy

The ratio of national debt to GDP was as high as 119 percent in 2011, although Italy, the third largest economy in the euro zone, had savings to purchase up to 57 percent of the national debt. As of July 12, 2012, Moody's reduced the national credit rating from A3 to Baa2 and warned about a further downgrade on the grounds of low economic growth, high unemployment, massive fiscal deficits, and unpopular national bonds and bills for foreign investors. S&P reduced the credit rating of Italy in September 2011, the first downgrade since 2006. There were rumors that Italy would be next in line, leading to existential questions about the fate of the EMU and eventually the EU.

2. Greece

The overall status of the Greek economy (September 2011) is self-explanatory by the following indexes: external debt/GDP (152.0 percent), fiscal deficit/GDP (8.7 percent), national debt/GDP (157.0 percent), economic growth (–4.5 percent), unemployment (16.0 percent), current account deficit (32.1 billion dollars), and S&P credit rating (CC).

Note that the pattern is very similar to that of Argentina at the time of its default in 2001. On July 1, 2011, the ECB approved an emergency aid tranche of twelve billion euros (17 billion dollars). It was the second three-year emergency aid package for Greece. The IMF helped remove the threat of default after the Greek Parliament passed laws for austerity.

3. Spain

After being mired in the euro zone's debt crisis for two-and-a-half years, Spain agreed to demands from its euro zone partners that it limit its budget deficit in 2012 to 5.3 percent of GDP.[7] However, Spain reached the point where it required a bailout following the one for Greece. Again, the problem was the collapse in the real estate market due to excessive loans and diminished regulatory oversight.

The IMF assessed that, although Spanish banks needed at least 50 billion dollars in additional capital to stabilize a deep economic downturn, major banks were well managed and appeared resilient to further shocks, although smaller banks were vulnerable.[8] Spain obtained an emergency fund of 100 billion euros in June 2012. There were rumors that Italy would be next in line, leading to existential questions about the fate of the EMU and eventually the EU.

5.4 IMPACT OF THE U.S. FINANCIAL CRISIS ON EAST ASIAN ECONOMY

The combined GDP of East Asia (including China, Japan and Korea) is approximately 20 percent of the world's total. If India and other emerging countries are included, the GDP figure for the Asian economy is much larger. According to the world economy projections (July 16, 2012) by the IMF, the impact of the U.S. financial crisis on the Asian economy is considerable, as expected under an open global system. The Japanese economy was already in recession. China's economy is no longer growing as rapidly as it used to. Korea is experiencing a tough time amid global stagnation. India and other emerging countries in Asia are all sluggish. Their economic performance, in turn, adversely affects the U.S. and European economies.

This section focuses on the impact of the U.S. financial crisis on Japan and China.

1. Japan

The Japanese economy was the second largest in the world before China emerged and has now become the third largest.[9] After magnificent growth and prosperity for several decades after World War II, it began to decline, especially after the failures in massive U.S. real estate investment during the 1990s. Japan also began to experience an economic crisis and political turmoil in 2007. The latest recession started in the last quarter of 2008. A series of ominous events occurred successively, including a subprime mortgage crisis and sluggish growth of GDP; the Nikkei average plummeted, then the U.S. export market was overtaken by China. GDP growth continued to slow down, despite the first fiscal stimulus of 11,500 billion yen, interest rates reduced to 0.03 percent, followed by another fiscal stimulus of 5,000 billion yen; the Nikkei and yen continued to fluctuate. Finally, Japan entered the first of seven years of recession. The latest recession occurred during the last quarter of 2008. Japan became a country of huge debt. The amounts of debt and annual interest payments are over 950 and 22 trillion yen (equivalent to 24 percent of the Japanese annual budget), respectively.

In addition to these cyclical problems, Japan has other chronic issues: a huge amount of idle savings unconverted into investment due to the austere Japanese lifestyle based on traditional virtues. There is also an increase in welfare spending for an aging population with a reputation for long life expectancy. The enormous amount of public expenditure for recovery from the tsunami and nuclear disasters of 2011 further increased the national debt. The decision to shut downs all fifty nuclear generators requires Japan to provide additional expenditure to secure energy from alternative sources. In order to control its growing debt, the Japanese government attempted to stimulate the economy numerous times by spending 124 trillion yen plus a monetary expansion of two trillion yen. However, the government spending only raised the national debt to a GDP ratio from 70 percent in 1990, to 140 in 2000, 212 in 2011, 230 in 2012, and to a higher percentage expected in the future due to massive increases in military spending scheduled by the Abe administration. It is unlikely that Japan will overcome its debt crisis in the near future. Amid its economic problems, a new nationalism has emerged in Japan. Such a dangerous political trend is causing political tensions, as substantiated by ongoing territorial disputes with China, Korea, and Russia.

Following are the rates of economic growth of Japan for 25 years in the past: 1980s (4.6 percent), 1990s (1.2), and 2000s (0.7). These numbers clearly suggest how rapidly the Japanese economy precipitated over time.

2. China

Since China became a member of the WTO in 2001, its economy has rapidly grown to the rank of second largest in the world. Its gross national income (GNI) as released by the OECD, increased from 1,169 billion dollars in 2000 to 4,856 billion dollars in 2009. In terms of rate of GDP per capita, it increased from 0.1 per cent in 2000 to 10.3 per cent in 2010 (See table 2.2 in chapter 2.) Given a population of 1.34 billion, however, per capita income is still very low. China has come a long way to become a member of the WTO but still has many years to go for a membership in the OECD, the group of advanced countries.[10] It also faces the dilemma of a large aging population that lacks a long-run social safety net. For example, the mass exodus of rural people to large cities for factory jobs has left many parents without adequate support in old age.

In any event, there have been significant changes in the global economy over the past decade. It is reasonable to suggest that the shift of global economic weight toward China is a primary cause of unprecedented economic incidents today, including global financial crises.

Major holders of U.S. government debt are China, Japan, and the United Kingdom. As of September 2008, China (585.0 billion dollars) overtook

Japan (573.2). U.S. securities are held primarily by China and Japan, 1.150 trillion and 1.117 trillion dollars, respectively, as of July 2012. In the *Economic Report of the President 2011*, the Council of Economic Advisors focused on statistical trends of U.S.-owned assets abroad, foreign-owned assets in the United States and U.S. Treasury securities during the period of 2005–2010. As discussed in chapter 3 of this book, government debt is not independent of trade deficits. In addition to the upward trends of U.S. trade deficits with respect to China, the U.S. trade imbalance is predominantly skewed toward East Asia, including Korea, and other Asian countries. Among Asian countries, China and Japan are two countries with enormous amounts of trade surplus against the United States. Over the past three decades, especially after becoming a member of the WTO, China has frequently achieved double-digit rates of economic growth. Its average annual rate of growth for the period until the global crisis was 9.5 percent. While the United States, Europe, and Japan have been mired in debt crises, China has been one of the few countries that have routinely outperformed growth projections. It is notable that China's exports to the United States exceeded Japan's largest amount of exports to the United States in August 2007. Such a remarkable growth boosted China to the status of second largest economy in the world. Heavy investment in housing and infrastructure during the period of 2009–2010 resulted in a peak of output growth in China, although its growth rate declined a little in 2009–2010, compared to 2008.

Slow growth with high unemployment in the United States and the EU, including the euro zone, and their interactive feedings began to pull China, India, and other major developing countries toward long-term stagnations. In early 2009, China's economy showed signs of a downturn, along with underlying problems:

- weakness in infrastructure for international competition, despite fast growth within a short period of time;
- increases in wages that eliminate comparative advantage;[11]
- a large, restive migration from agricultural to urban areas and a high rate of unemployment;
- environmental problems exacerbated by rapid growth;
- social problems associated with fast urbanization;
- problems of income distribution in the absence of a middle-income bracket.

There have been debates among policy makers in China about the priority of growth versus stability, including the possibility of a hard landing for an overheated future Chinese economy. In general, a majority of policy makers in China are optimistic about achieving a sustained growth rate of 8 percent, whereas foreign research institutes have projected it in the range of 5–7.5 percent. The desired rate by China is 7–8 percent at least. Former premier Wen Jiabao set the annual target rate of growth for

2012 at 7.5 percent. The fiscal deficit was expected to grow to 3 percent of GDP, estimated as 950 billion yuan. However, actual growth was only 7 percent as of July 2012. Investment spending reached its saturation point, and exports, housing, manufacturing, retail, and all of other leading indicators showed downward movement. In addition, other Asian economies slowed down. Relatively developed economies like those of Korea and Taiwan and rapidly developing countries like India and Brazil were also on the downhill side of growth rates.

The IMF chief economist, Olivier Blanchard, recently predicted that the world economy would enter a dangerous new phase.[12] Robert Zoellick, former president of the World Bank, suggested that their current growth model was not optimistic about the future of China's economy. The Asian Development Bank (ADB) projected the average rate of economic growth of the fast-growing Asian countries, China and India, to be as low as 6.5 percent. In his book, Sharma (2012) suggests that China will experience a natural slowdown. His rationale is interesting. Economic growth by means of government spending on depreciating infrastructure results in a larger economy with a larger middle-income bracket, thus higher savings rates, and a larger aging population to support.

NOTES

1. The European Common Agriculture Policy was often controversial among agricultural countries, including the United States.

2. See Chung (2006) for trade disputes between European Countries and the United States. The number of disputes between the United States and EU is the largest.

3. See Hook's Law on vibrational motion in physics.

4. See the *Financial Times*, Tuesday November 25, 2008, p. 13.

5. In order to protect the global economy from the euro zone debt crisis, the G-20 and emerging economies pledged 430 billion dollars in new funding for the IMF's lending facility on April 20, 2012. The amount of new funding, the IMF's existing resources, and the committed loan amount add up to one trillion dollars, an amount believed to be enough for the IMF to respond to debt problems in any country and region. See http://news.yahoo.com/g20-doubles-imfs-war-chest-amid-fears-europe-010053830--business---, accessed April 21, 2012.

6. Jenes Weidmann , president of the Bundesbank, asked Mario Draghi to withdraw exceptional help for euro zone banks and to review risks taken by the ECB. *Financial Times*, March 14, 2012. See Zakaria, Fareed, "The Savior of Europe," *Time*, March 12, 2012, p.18.

7. *Financial Times*, March 14, 2012.

8. *Washington Post*, June 9, 2012.

9. The Smithsonian Agreement and the Plaza Agreement in the 1970s and 1980s were basically concerned with yen at the peak time of the Japanese economy.

10. See chapter 2 for the passage on China with the United States' endorsement in order to become a member of the WTO.

11. In his article on Chinese philosophy for innovation, Davis (2012) argues that technological innovation will need to become more important in order to increase the productivity of labor and to hold down increases in wages in the future if China expects to maintain high rates of economic growth.

12. IMF, *World Economic Outlook*, 2005–2013.

III

Origins of Global Economic Disparities

SIX

Human Resources and Technology

In the 1960s and 1970s, the Cobb-Douglas and the constant-elasticity-of-substitution (CES) production functions were popular in connection with studies on income distribution. The primary objective of a production function was to confirm whether the output shares of capital (the share to the upper-level income bracket) and labor (the share to the low income bracket) add up to unity (or 100 percent). In terms of the elasticity of substitution, however, the two functions are rigid. They are restricted to unity and constant, respectively. Since the oil crises in the 1970s, energy has become an important productive factor. In 1973, the transcendental logarithmic (translog) production function was introduced. Unlike the previous two functions, the translog function is flexible. The Allen-Uzawa partial elasticities of substitution (AES) for any pair of inputs are not constant like the earlier production functions. The flexibility of this function has allowed energy and materials as inputs in addition to capital and labor.

The purpose of this chapter is not to conduct cross-country studies of production functions but to explore global disparities in human resources and the corresponding economic arguments in the GED-GHE proposition addressed in this book. Although labor is the central component of human resources, it is not directly relevant to this chapter. Among all inputs, labor is the essential factor. Even without the other productive factors, the basic economy in a country can still prevail only with labor. However, labor is internationally immobile. The Heckscher-Ohlin-Samuelson theory (HOS) characterized in terms of factor endowment and factor intensity presupposes of immobility of labor. In the real world today, labor in a country is not separable from capital and technology in other countries that are mobile. Foreign direct investment is globally significant today. Multinational corporations (MNCs) of capital-abundant countries (developed countries including superpowers) transfer human capital (education, job training, and health embodied workers) along with technologies to labor-abundant countries where wages are relatively low.[1] Such a human capital–augmented labor is referred to as "human resources," the primary argument in this chapter.

Actual data for human resources, their productivities and hourly compensations are available only for a limited number of even OECD countries. Hourly wages and productivities in other countries such as China and India are not available. However, the rationale for lower wages in populous underdeveloped countries, in comparison with those in developed countries, is sufficient in this chapter. Although the HOS theory is not directly relevant here, the factor-price equalization theorem, a subset of the HOS, suggests that low wages in underdeveloped countries increase steadily over time in the long run.

MNCs transfer technologies to foreign countries through their FDIs. They are giant corporations such as ExxonMobil, Royal Dutch, BP, GM, Toyota, Daimler Chrysler, Mitsbushi, GE, Ford, and Siemens. Their annual sales are enormous. Percentages of their foreign sales are mostly above 50 percent of total sales. There has been a rapid development in the area of telecommunication and electronic devices for the past fifty years. Samsung Electronics, Hewlett Packard, Apple, IBM-USA, Sony, Dell, Intel, and Nokia developed magnificent technologies. Their sales range from about 50 million to 150 million dollars and the number of employees ranges from 50,000 to 200,000. Innovation through R&D requires entrepreneurs to train and educate workers to produce new products by new processes over time. Various software and IT systems provided by such companies as Microsoft, Google, MacIntosh, and so on, have restructured all areas in the labor-saving manner. MNCs' FDIs of developed countries are powerful driving forces for production of new products in the world market.[2] There are even species of homegrown technological products and business innovation in India and China. They involve types of re-engineering high-tech products or a decentralized approach to technological products and business innovation.[3]

In brief, ubiquitous integrals between the physical domain and cyberspace change the entire world today. Large firms develop new technologies and produce new products. They make radical departures from the traditional mode of human life. Global disparities in knowledge and information and choices of digital-oriented consumers determine their future. Massive unemployment released by the losers becomes a serious concern in the future.

6.1 HUMAN RESOURCES: AN OVERVIEW

Table 6.1 exhibits basic data for human resources of selected countries. They are the data available *consistently from the same source*: U.S. Census Bureau, *Statistical Abstract of the United States 2012*, the latest version as of now.

The total population in less-developed countries (LDCs) is larger than that in developed countries, with a concentration of 82 percent of the world's total in Asia, Africa, and South America. A high concentration in Asia is attributable to the extremely large populations of China and India. Among the developed countries, the United States and Japan are relatively more populous than developed countries in Europe. Although the sizes of the labor force in many LDCs (not listed in the table) are not available, they should be proportional to their populations. Wages in LDCs are also unavailable. However, it is a matter of fact that hourly compensation in developed countries is much higher than those in LDCs. Rates of unemployment in developed countries are high. Figures for LDCs are unknown but supposed to be high across countries. High unemployment rates across the world imply that the global economy as a whole is sluggish or there are too many people living in the world compared to available jobs. Overall, global disparities (GED) in human resources among developed countries (superpowers) are considerable, and GEDs between developed countries and LDCs are serious.

"Human resource" is a comprehensive term. Human resources are divided into unskilled and skilled workers. A majority of workers in a country are unskilled. Unlike skilled labor, unskilled labor is uneducated. Their work is monotonous. They receive low wages. Unskilled workers represent the low income bracket and thus are generally at the bottom of the class structure, almost always at the poverty level. However, they are the ones who attract MNCs' investment from developed countries and MNCs educate and train them for access to new technologies, simply their capital (stock of investment). Of course, there are in many cases domestic firms that develop technologies jointly with foreign multinational corporations. Except for a small number of labor-intensive industries (e.g., textile and apparel), such a fusion between labor and capital, namely *capital-technology augmented labor*, reduces the significance of manual workers these days unless there is a special purpose for particular research on production technology in a country.

The next section provides the rationale for an integral factor of capital and labor. Such a view is the underlying basis that justifies the arguments presented in this chapter.

Table 6.1.   Population, Civilian Labor Force, Unemployment, and Hourly Compensation

	Population[a]	Labor Force[b]	Unemployment[c]	Hourly Compensation[d]
Africa	1,015			
S. Africa	49			
Asia	4,133			
China	1,330			
India	1,173			
Japan	127	65	5	91
Korea, S.	43		4	42
Europe	734			
France	65	28	9	120
Germany	83	41	7	139
Italy	58	25	8	104
Russia	139			
U.K.	62	31	8	92
North America	539			
U.S.	310	154	10	100
Canada	34	18	8	88
Mexico	113			*16*
South America	396			
Argentina	41			30
Brazil	201			*25*
Oceania	35			
Australia	24	12	5	103
LDC's (percent)	82			
Developed (percent)	18			
World (193 countries)	6,853			

Notes:

a Population: million, 2010

b Labor force: Civilian labor force; U.S., Canada, France, and U.K., 16 years; Japan, Germany, and Italy, 15 years, 2010.

c Unemployment: Annual average percentage rate, 2010.

d Indexes of hourly compensation costs for all employees in manufacturing by country, 2009.

Sources:
1. U.S. Census Bureau, *Statistical Abstract of the United States*: 2012, pp. 836–38.
2. Ibid., p. 856.
3. Ibid, p. 849.

6.2 TECHNOLOGICAL INNOVATION

Joseph A. Schumpeter (1883–1950) asserted that innovation is critical for economic change, entrepreneurship and market power.[4] Entrepreneurs (in developed countries or superpowers) constantly disturb the Walrasian equilibrium; and thus, their random disturbances or external shocks in general are the prime motivator of economic development. Its time path follows a cyclical pattern.[5]

The low wages of the massive labor force in China, for example, have recently induced investment in technology from multinational corporations. In the long run, however, wages in China are expected to be higher. As mentioned previously, there is a theory, referred to as the Heckscher-Ohlin-Samuelson theory (HOS), suggesting that the labor-abundant country specializes production of labor-intensive commodity, the capital-abundant country specializes production of a capital-intensive commodity, and the two countries trade them for mutual advantage. As a subset of the HOS, the factor-price equalization suggests that factor prices are equalized across the countries in the long run in the competitive open economy.[6] Technology transfers that require multinational corporations to educate and train unskilled workers should be another reason for higher wages in China in addition to the simple law of supply and demand. Higher wages received by skilled labor embodied with technology eliminate comparative advantage in the international market.[7] Although some argue that wages in China are no longer low, the inflection point of high wages requires taking into account the fact that the average level of hourly wages in China is still relatively low in comparison with those in developed countries, and technology reduces the production cost.

In the real world, where multinational corporations are active, labor in one country is virtually inseparable from capital in another country. New production processes for new products manufactured by firms as a result of their R&D and innovation, whether they are intellectual property rights or high-technology communication devices, require workers to take up education and training, that is, a firm's investment for human resources. Skilled labor is simply an investment-augmented labor.

Capital-technology augmented labor applied to the open economy system in this chapter is based on Schumpeter's theory of innovation. It is a valid concept for quality of labor rather than the size of workforce.

6.3 FOREIGN DIRECT INVESTMENT AND HUMAN CAPITAL

In the conventional framework of economics, labor and capital are two distinctive primary inputs for the production of outputs. As discussed in the previous section, technological innovation turns the two separable factors into virtually one integral input. Technologies transferred internationally through foreign direct investment of multinational corporations facilitate the integral process. Labor incorporated with knowledge, education, training, skills, and experience is characterized as a capital-technology augmented labor.

By definition, foreign direct investment is long-term investment with controlling interests of investors in foreign countries, where the long-term is a period longer than one year and controlling interests mean 10 percent (15 percent in the United States) or more ownership. In comparison with the stock market for portfolio investments, FDI is stable by nature. In general, FDI is an investment behavior of giant corporations in developed countries. They are mostly multinational corporations that operate in one or more foreign country through affiliates or subsidiaries. There are many arguments for and against FDI between a source country and a host country. Though not directly relevant to be discussed here, typical arguments include questions about tax evasion in the source country and actual technology transfers in the host country.

Multinational corporations are mostly oligopolists in each corresponding industry from the microeconomics standpoint, and each oligopolist is not significantly different from the monopolist because the technology developed at the firm level is unique to the firm or the corresponding industry. A few large companies have resources and capital to invest in R&D for an industrial sector.[8] A new technology stimulates the incentive to develop new products and production processes for investment in a foreign country where wages are low. However, the market power of innovation is inter-temporal. It will soon be competed away by rivals. There will also be close substitutes in the market. In the electronic and audiovisual industries, for example, there have been the actual transitions from radios to transistor radios, black and white TVs to color TVs, LCD to LED, and so on. Competition in electronic communication devices, such as cell phones and tablets, between Apple and Samsung and now the 3D printer revolution are the areas of the latest competition.[9] Real world develops in accordance with Schumpeterian thought.

It is important to stress that labor and capital, the two primary productive inputs, are not separable in the actual production process today because new products and new production processes and facilities require highly skilled workers who are trained for applications of new technologies.

Table 6.2 shows the FDIs of ten countries selected from twenty-nine OECD nations. The amounts of their inflows and outflows are enormous.

A considerable portion of each amount represents technologies transferred by multinational corporations (entrepreneurs) of developed foreign countries. FDIs in the United States by other developed countries and FDIs in other developed countries by the United States have considerably increased, especially in Europe and Asia. Table 6.3 exhibits FDIs by industry from the rest of the world (ROW) to the U.S. and from the United States to the ROW in 2000 and 2009. Their amounts remained almost the same in 2000. However, FDIs by both after a decade increased substantially and the FDI by the United States is significantly larger than that by the ROW. FDI for the manufacturing sector by the United States (2010) was smaller than that by the ROW (2009), whereas FDI for finance and insurance by the Ubuted States considerably larger than that by the ROW.

It is important to keep in mind that the FDIs in the areas of (a) computer and electronic services in manufacturing, (b) information and professional and (c) scientific and technological services are directly relevant to MNCs' investment involved with technologies transferred to LDCs. Though not extremely large, the total amount of FDI in these sectors is significant in the sense that the information-technology-oriented world economy of today would collapse in the absence of these particular industrial sectors.

Table 6.4 presents the number of employees and capital expenditures of U.S. non-bank MNCs.

Table 6.2. Foreign Direct Investment Flows of OECD Countries (Cumulative 1990–2009, in billions of dollars)

	Inflows	Outflows
Canada	514.8	558.2
France	806.0	1,514.5
Germany	735.6	1,125.2
Japan	219.4	1,032.5
Luxembourg	1,016.4	1,167.5
Mexico	290.3	NA
Netherlands	525.8	824.0
Spain	468.1	685.3
Switzerland	201.2	516.2
U.K.	1,252.5	1,723.2
U.S.	2,689.8	2,908.8

Source: U.S. Census Bureau, *Statistical Abstract of the United States*: 2012, p. 876.

Table 6.3.　Foreign Direct Investment by Industry (in billions of dollars)

	FDI in the U.S.		FDI by the U.S.	
	2000	2009	2000	2009
Total	1,357	2,115	1,316	3,908
Manufacturing		748[a]	344	586
Computer and Electronic				
Services			60	82
Information			52	162
Professional, Scientific,				
And Technical Services			33	85
Finance and Insurance		357[b]	217	803

Source: U.S. Census Bureau, *Statistical Abstract of the United States*:
　　2012, p. 797 and p. 799.
　　Notes:
　　[a, b] Figures for 2010.

Over thirty million employees have been hired by both U.S. parent companies and majority-owned foreign affiliates. The amount of their capital expenditures is over 700 billion dollars. The total number of employees and the total amount of capital expenditures of all countries are undoubtedly very large. Tables 6.5 is concerned with key global telecom indicators: fixed telephone lines, mobile cellular subscribers, Internet users, fixed broadband subscribers, and mobile broadband subscribers. The number of fixed telephone line subscribers decreased significantly over a period of five years in the recent past, whereas mobile cellular and broadband subscribers increases dramatically. The number of mobile cellular subscribers and Internet users in developed countries has almost doubled in five years. For the data on telephone main lines, cellular phone subscribers and Internet users (in percent of population), see the same data source for table 6.5. These are the key telecommunication devices of high technology used in the globalized business world today.

Table 6.4. Employees and Capital Expenditures of U.S. Nonbank Multinational Corporations

	Employees (thousands)		Capital Expenditures (billions of dollars)	
	2000	2009	2000	2009
Parents and MOFAs	32,057	31,227	548	658
Parents	23,885	21,103	438	479

Note: MOFA = Majority-owned foreign affiliate.
Source: U.S. Census Bureau, *Statistical Abstract of the United States*: 2012, p. 519.

6.4 R&D AND PATENTS

Innovation is the prime cause of economic growth and development. It requires investment in R&D for new technologies. R&D enhances opportunities for new patents, inventions, and designs. These reshape the world with new products and services.

New technologies improve not only the efficiency of production processes but also create high-technology-embodied new products for consumers in the world market. New products can significantly change the lifestyle of consumers, as exemplified by the many recent new products in the area of communication and information technology.

In general, innovation and technological progress take place mostly in developed countries where R&D expenditures are high. GDP expenditure on R&D in developed countries is mostly high. Figure 6.1 shows rations of R&D expenditure with respect to GDP for each of the selected OECD countries of relatively high growth rates. Countries that spend relatively small amounts on R&D are Brazil, China, India, Mexico, and Russia. These countries are not included in the figure 6.1. However, their potential, especially that of China and India should not be underestimated. Although data for higher education expenditures on R&D are not available, these should generally be proportional to total GDP expenditure for R&D. It is notable that the R&D expenditure made by South Korea, a small but developed country, is larger than expenditures made by France, Germany, Japan, and the United States.

The primary purpose of R&D expenditure by a country is inventions and new product designs and ultimately to obtain patents domestically and internationally. Figure 6.2 shows U.S. patents granted to residents of

Table 6.5.   Key Global Telecom Indicators for the World Telecommunications Service Sector (in millions)

Indicators	2005	2010
Fixed Telephone Lines	1,259	1,197
Mobil Cellular Subscribers	2,278	5,282
Internet Users	1,036	2,084
Fixed Broadband Subscribers	216	555
Mobile Broadband Subscribers	73	940

Source: U.S. Census Bureau, *Statistical Abstract of the United States*, 2012, p.868.

foreign countries in 2010 in order of the number of patents. R&D expenditures and the number of patents are roughly correlated. Countries with large amounts of R&D expenditure and numbers of patents are developed or fast growing. Finally, note that the number of patents obtained by Japan is exceedingly large. Germany obtains a larger return in terms of number of patents in comparison with its R&D expenditure.

There are several critiques of the global trend toward technological innovation:

1. Innovation and technology intensify competition among advanced countries for raw materials in natural resource–abundant underdeveloped countries. Competition for raw materials among developed countries (superpowers) is historically a well-known subject of foreign policies and geopolitics.
2. Information technology facilitates financial transactions among global financial centers, encourages speculative activities, and may result in financial crises.
3. Innovation stimulates international trade and may result in trade wars and disputes over infringements of the intellectual property of one country by another country.
4. Multinational corporations, including high-technology developers, are motivated to invest in foreign countries partly because cheap labor is available. Their investments abroad increase unemployment in home countries.

There are pros and cons for each of the critiques. Although it is not the objective of this chapter to discuss such specific arguments, our own generation has witnessed new production techniques attributable to mi-

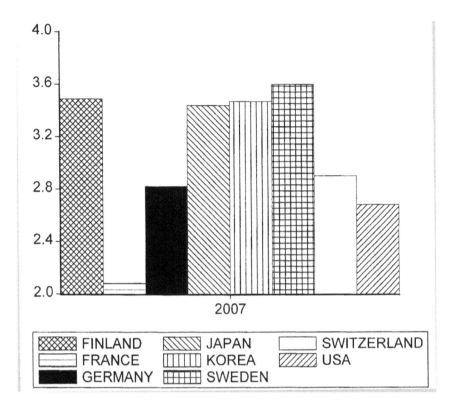

Figure 6.1.   R and D Expenditures by Country (percent of GDP). Note: R and D figures for France and Germany in 2009. Data: U.S. Census Bureau, Statistical Abstract of the United States: 2012, Washington, D.C.: U.S. GPO, p. 874.

raculous advancements in the area of high technology. A new technology that evolves from innovation in a given country reduces the degrees of economic disparity for certain countries but increases the degrees of disparity with other countries. According to Schumpeter, innovation is cyclical. Then the disparity should become circular.[10] Unless innovation takes place constantly and concurrently over time in all countries, disturbances such as a trade surplus in a country generated from innovation do not readily gravitate to an equilibrium situation. Questions about the amplitudes and durations of circular disparities complicate the argument further. Although irrelevant here, their magnitudes should depend on the type of innovation. They also depend on the intensity of interactions among global economies and the degree of vibrations induced from them. Such an irregular nature of innovation generates global economic disparities (GEDs) in virtually all market areas. Irrespective of existing theories of business cycles, it is difficult for (developed) countries to nor-

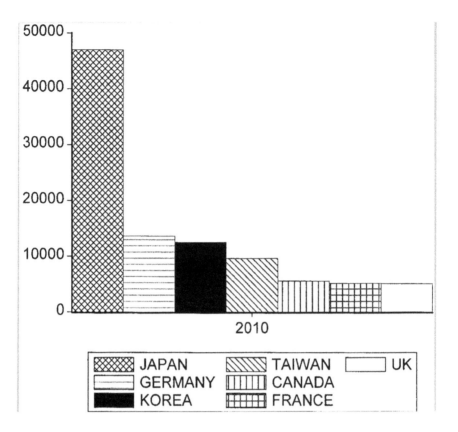

Figure 6.2. Patents by Country Note: Includes only U.S. patents granted to residents of areas outside of the United States. Data: U.S. Census Bureau, Statistical Abstract of the United States: 2012, Washington, D.C.: U.S. GPO, p. 868.

malize a global economic disparity in the real world when innovation takes place successively but irregularly.

In conclusion, different countries have different kinds of human capital. They are not synchronized. Human capital in one country may be more advanced than in another. Innovation associated with human capital is clearly a source of global economic disparities in the real world that perpetuates geoeconomic competition among superpowers.

NOTES

1. Multinational corporations (MNCs) are firms that own and operate production facilities in foreign countries. They are giant corporations well-known in the world, as published in magazines.

2. Numerical data in this section have been obtained from media sources.

3. In his article (2012) on China's new, cheaper, and simplified homegrown innovation for their low-income consumers, Gary Davis argues that technological innova-

tion will need to become more important in order to increase labor productivity and to hold down increases in wages in the future.

4. See Schumpeter (1949). Robert Solow (1956), the Nobel Laureate in Economics in 1987 for his contributions on the theory of economic growth, expanded Schumpeter's theory and expounded technological innovations that dictate that the world economy today can be labor saving, capital saving, or neutral.

5. There are four different cycles: Kitchin inventory (3–5 years), Juglar inventory (7–11), Kuznets investment (15–25), and Kondratief cycle (45–60). The cyclical path suggested by Schumpeter was a general pattern of cycle rather than a specific dynamic path over time as described here.

6. The Heckscher-Ohlin-Samuelson theory is the modern theory of international trade, a dominant part of international economics.

7. MNCs' investment causes often geoeconomic controversy between a source country and a host country. In August 2008, the United States withdrew investment from Russia due to a political crisis in Georgia.

8. Schumpeter, Joseph A., "Economic Theory and Entrepreneurial History," *Change and Entrepreneur*, 1949.

9. 3D printer revolution is a term representing digitation of manufacturing-mass customization with software, robots, new technology-embodied materials and production procedures.

10. For such a perspective on innovations, cycles, and development, see his work (1954), *The Theory of Economic Development*. In his empirical test of a technology-embodied production function, Professor Robert Solow (1956) confirmed a significantly larger proportion of output attributed to the technological innovation than to labor and capital.

SEVEN
Raw Materials

Abundant coal, iron, and other basic materials in England contributed to the onset of the first industrial revolution in the eighteenth century. In turn, the second industrial revolution in England and succeeding industrial revolutions over time in other Western European countries, including France, Italy, and Germany, required them to secure raw materials from overseas. As a result, imperialism emerged. Coercive practices of European countries to achieve extractive economic objectives in their colonies were widespread in Asia and Africa for much of the nineteenth century.[1] In the relentless pursuit of raw materials and oil during World War II, Japan also learned how useful imperialism could be to their economy by invading neighboring countries in East and Southeast Asia.

Raw materials are indispensable for the production of finished goods. However, their amounts on earth are fixed, and most of their deposits are concentrated in certain areas and countries. Given the uneven endowments of raw materials, the GED argument in this area is viable. It is natural to expect that conflicts of interest among producing and consuming countries will occur. There are many geoeconomic implications associated with their strategies in market processes. In the past, many underdeveloped countries, often former Western colonies, have complained of exploitation by developed countries. As raw materials become scarcer and their prices higher, industrial countries endeavor to secure raw materials (and energy) almost anywhere in the world. Attempts to expand their exclusive zones for maritime resources also become more aggressive today, even in the Arctic Ocean and Antarctica.

This chapter presents economic perspectives on raw materials and examines endowments of natural resources in the world, primary producing countries, and prices of selected raw materials in the world market. There is considerable GED in the area of raw materials. The geoeconomic implications of natural resources are highlighted.

7.1 PERSPECTIVES ON RAW MATERIALS IN ECONOMICS

There is no doubt that raw materials are important productive factors, like capital and labor. However, economists have ignored them under the assumption that raw materials are mathematically "constant or fixed" in the production function, presumably for two reasons: First, the primary purpose of the production function was to investigate income distribution between the upper-level income bracket (capital) and the lower-level income bracket (labor) at the time when the production function was introduced in economics. Therefore, it was sufficient for researchers to take into account the two productive factors, capital and labor, in the production function. Second, the rigidity associated with the production function in terms of the elasticity of substitution was restricted to unity or a constant. These restrictions eliminate *a priori* theoretical and empirical significance for consideration of additional inputs like raw materials and energy in the production function.

This section briefly reviews production functions and justifies raw materials as meaningful inputs in flexible production functions. The theoretical part discussed in this section is also applicable to the subsequent chapter on energy.

The Cobb-Douglas and the CES (constant elasticity of substitution) production functions were introduced by Cobb and Douglas in 1928 and Arrow, Chenery, Minhas, and Solow in 1961, respectively. Economists employed both functions extensively for their empirical research in the 1960s and 1970s. However, there are fundamental rigidities associated with these two popular neoclassical production functions. Homotheticity and (quasi-) additivity are the underlying assumptions imposed on each of the production functions that result in (a) the Allen-Uzawa partial elasticities of substitution (AES) restricted to unity or constant, and (b) the factor shares of output are constant and independent of output. In particular, the AES restricted to unity or any constant number is a serious weakness of these two production functions in the absence of important policy implications. In both cases of production functions, it is not really meaningful to take into account additional inputs because they yield simply another constant AESs for any pair of inputs with materials or energy.

The magnitude of AES determines the degree of effectiveness of a pricing policy. It is important to have a flexible production function that provides information on variable factor substitutions between any pair of productive factors in economics. Christensen, Jorgenson and Lau (1973) introduced the transcendental logarithmic (translog) production function that does not impose homotheticity and separability. The AESs and output shares of inputs are not *a priori* restricted to any particular number.[2] The translog function is a flexible production function that accommodates any number of inputs. The function has advanced to a more sophisticated version of the translog, the CES-translog production function. The translog function emerged long after Professor Leontief (the Nobel Laureate in Economics in 1973) introduced the Input-Output Table in 1953, a representation of production technology of *fixed* input coefficients for each industry. This is a massive table that determines projected output in each sector of industries in order to meet the desired final demand (household consumption, fixed capital formation, government expenditures, increases or decreases of inventories and net exports) that is determined by policy makers.[3] The translog function has relaxed the rigidity imposed on the existing neoclassical production functions. The Shephard duality theorem (the one-to-one correspondence between output and cost for a particular production technology) and the Shephard lemma (the theoretical basis for price dynamics in connection with *all* factor prices) incorporated with the translog function have provided the theoretical basis for empirical studies done on raw materials within the context of the production function.[4]

As countries, both developed and developing, continue to pursue industrialization of their economies, they compete to secure raw materials virtually everywhere in the world. As raw materials become scarcer, their prices increase. However, there was virtually no rigorous study that focused on the causality of material costs on inflation until the latter part of 1970s. Serious concerns about inflation began with the oil crises, coincidentally with material costs. A research study strongly confirms the significance of inflationary effects of materials costs.[5] The relationship between prices of materials and the price of a finished good recognizes raw materials as important inputs in the production function.

There are a few other views that explain why countries continue to demand more materials:

- As science and technology advance, raw materials became increasingly important. At present, there are almost invisible wars going on between countries in pursuit of specific materials in certain industrial sectors. For example, industrial countries are desperately seeking land-scarce materials for their high-technology industries (e.g., rare earth materials)
- Demographers have concerns about the world's capacity of providing natural resources in the future. Kunzig (2011) suggests that, since global population grows by 80 million a year, total world population will rise from seven billion people in 2011 to nine billion by 2045. There will be serious shortages in natural resources as population increases.[6]

The endowment of factors plays a key role in the modern theory of international trade. This theory, often referred to as the Heckscher-Ohlin-Samuelson theory (HOS), states that a country exports an abundant-factor-intensive good and imports a scarce-factor-intensive good. Under *competitive* free trade, factor prices, both wages and rental cost, are equalized in the long run. In such a case of automatic adjustment to global equilibrium, the factor-price equalization theorem is valid, and the global economic disparity (GED) in the area of raw materials is not a viable argument. However, the amounts of raw materials on earth are fixed and most of their deposits are unevenly endowed. Furthermore, the industrial structure of developed countries is imperfectly competitive. Large firms with increasing returns to scale produce slightly differentiated products. Product differentiation naturally results in intra-industry trade. The trade pattern in industrialized countries is predominantly intra-industrial. European countries (such as the U.K., France, Germany, and Italy) and the North American countries (the United States, Canada, and Mexico) are the countries of heavy intra-industry trade; intra-industry trade among Asian countries (Korea, China, and Japan) is also considerable. In terms of product category, organic and inorganic chemicals, potash, dynamite, and iron and steel are monopolistically competitive in the case of the United States.[7] Professor Stigler (1947) included nonferrous metal (aluminum and copper) and steel industries in the oligopolistic category. It is unreasonable to presuppose that the GED argument is not viable on the Heckscher-Ohlin-Samuelson theory that is upheld in the long run.

7.2 ENDOWMENT AND PRODUCTION OF RAW MATERIALS BY COUNTRY

Unlike markets for capital and labor, two conventional factors, many raw materials are endowed in a limited number of countries. In addition, many countries own or directly control major raw materials. Capital is internationally mobile. Labor is strictly subject to the immigration and naturalization laws in each country but is regarded as a mobile factor from labor-abundant countries to labor-scarce countries in the long run. As discussed in the previous chapter, the foreign direct investment by MNCs plays an important role that affects the international labor market indirectly. International mobility of raw materials is similar to the case of labor. In comparison to the case of finished goods, there are considerable degrees of rigidity in markets of raw materials. More importantly, there are certain cases where the conventional laws of supply and demand are not applicable to raw materials. For example, China, a material-abundant country, keeps buying up raw materials around the world beyond the demand required for its rapid growth. According to a data base of the American Enterprise Institute (AEI) and the Heritage Foundation, overseas investment in resources by China increased from 8.2 billion dollars in 2005 to 53.3 billion dollars in 2013.[8]

Table 7.1 exhibits the status of endowments and production of metallic minerals and nonmetalic minerals in the world by country. Almost all of them are distributed unevenly among a limited number of countries or areas.

- Of the fourteen countries in the list, China has the most abundant mineral reserves of seven minerals ranked in the top three in terms of percentage of endowment. These are aluminum, copper, iron ore, lead, mercury, tin, and zinc. Australia, Canada, and Russia are also abundant in these seven minerals. China is also rich in supplies of minerals other than the nineteen minerals listed above. It is notable, for instance, that China possesses almost all of the rare earth minerals.
- In light of its territorial mass and global economic and political hegemony, the United States is a relatively metallic- mineral–scarce country. However, the United States is abundant in some nonmetallic minerals such as nitrogen, salt, and sulfur.
- European countries in general are not resource abundant.
- Japan, an economic superpower, is a resource-scarce country. Japan is listed with only five of nineteen metallic minerals.
- There are virtually no mineral endowments in the Middle East and North East Africa. Oil is the only resource that they have as of now.

Geoeconomic implications based on a few observations above are as follows: Shortages of raw materials in European countries and Japan explain at least partially the imperialistic histories of some European countries as well as Japan. The United States has also caused resentment from Latin American countries in connection with raw materials extraction in the past. Chances for market failure in raw materials are high even today. Accordingly, conflicts of interest between producing and consuming countries can be severe.

7.3 PRICES OF RAW MATERIALS IN THE WORLD MARKET

As the global economy grows rapidly, excess demand for raw materials in industrial countries increases their prices. Recently, China, a resource-abundant country, has aggressively imported enormous amounts of raw materials from all over the world and continues to look for them everywhere. China's trade surplus has gradually diminished over time. The amount of net imports (= imports–exports) of raw materials was 501.4 billion in 2011, an increase of 43.3 percent in comparison with trade defi-

Table 7.1.   Endowments and Production of Raw Materials

(1) Metallic Minerals

Aluminum	China (33.8 percent), Russia (9.7 percent), Canada (8.0 percent); Australia, Brazil, Norway, U.S.
Bauxite	Australia (29.9 percent), China (17.1 percent), Brazil (10.7 percent); Guyana, India, Jamaica, Russia, Suriname, U.S., Western Sahara
Chromium	South Africa (44.9 percent), Kazakhstan (17.1 percent), India (15.4 percent); Brazil
Copper	China (36.1 percent), Peru (7.7 percent), U.S. (7.6 percent); Argentina, Canada, Chile, Germany, Indonesia, Japan, Kazakhstan, Korea, Mexico, Philippines, Poland, Russia, South Africa, Zambia
Gold	China (11.8 percent), South Africa (10.8 percent), Australia (10.5 percent); Brazil, Canada, Papua New Guinea, Philippines, Russia, U.S.
Iron Ore	China (34.8 percent), Brazil (17.5 percent), Australia (14.7 percent); Canada, India, Korea, Mexico, Peru, Russia, Sweden, U.K., Ukraine, U.S., Venezuela
Lead	China (39.1 percent), Australia (16.8 percent), U.S. (10.7 percent); Canada, Germany, Greece, Japan, Kazakhstan, Mexico, Morocco, Peru, Spain, South Africa, Russia, Turkey, U.K.
Manganese	South Africa (20.6 percent), Australia (20.2 percent), China (15.9 percent); India, Turkey, Ukraine
Magnesite	China
Mercury	China (60.6 percent), Kyrgyzstan (18.9 percent); Finland, Mexico, Spain, Turkey, U.S.
Molybdenum	Canada, Chile, China, Korea, Mexico, Peru, Russia, U.S.
Nickel	Russia (16.9 percent), Canada (15.3 percent), Indonesia (13.8 percent); Australia, Brazil, Finland, Jamaica, Japan, South Africa, U.S.

Rare Earth Minerals	China (97 percent); Australia, Brazil, India, Malaysia, Russia, U.S.
Silver	Peru (16.6 percent), Mexico (14.2 percent), China (12.8 percent); Argentina, Australia, Chile, Japan, Ukraine, U.S.
Tin	China (41.4 percent), Indonesia (31.3 percent), Peru (12.0 percent); Brazil, Malaysia, Russia
Tungsten	Bolivia, China, Italy, Korea, Philippines, Portugal, Russia
Uranium	Canada (20 percent), Kazakhstan (19.4 percent), Australia (19.2 percent); China, Korea
Vanadium	China
Zinc	China (26.6 percent), Australia (13.9 percent), Peru (13.2 percent); Canada, Ireland, Kazakhstan, Korea, Japan, Mexico, Russia, Sweden, U.S.

(2) Nonmetallic minerals

Antimony	China
Cement	China, India, U.S.
Cobalt	Australia, Canada, Russia, Zimbabwe
Diamond	Australia, Belgium, Botswana, Brazil, Canada, Congo, India, Japan, Korea, Mexico, Namibia, Russia, South Africa, Sweden, Tanzania, U.K., U.S.
Graphite	Korea
Nitrates	Chile
Nitrogen	China, India, Russia, U.S., Morocco
Phosphate	Western Sahara
Potash	Canada, Belarus, Russia
Rubber	Argentina, Brazil, Congo, Malaysia, Sumatra
Salt	China, Germany, U.S.
Sulfur	China, Russia, U.S.

Note: Countries and numbers in parentheses are amounts of production by major producing countries.

Sources:

(1) Barraclough, Geoffrey (ed.), *The Times Atlas of World History*, sixth ed., London; Times Book, 1998, pp. 100-101.

(2) Oxford University Press, *Essential World Atlas*, sixth ed., London; Philip's, 2011, pp. 26-27.

(3) U.S. Census Bureau, *Statistical Abstract of the United States*: 2012, p. 862.

(4) http://www.Mapsofworld.com/world-mineral-map.htm. Accessed May 5, 2012.

cits in 2010. Given this trend, the future prices of raw materials in the world market remain to be seen.

Figure 7.1 exhibits average prices of five minerals (copper, iron, nickel, platinum, and tin) selected from nine major minerals (copper, platinum, nickel, tin, iron ore, gold, silver, lead, and zinc) for the period 1980–2010 with intervals of ten years.[9] For the first ten years (1980–1990), prices of platinum and tin decreased, whereas the price of nickel increased and prices of copper and iron ore remained constant. For the second ten years (1990–2000), prices of all five items remained almost constant. However, all prices, except the price of iron ore, increased sharply for the third ten years (2000–2010).

Except for gold and silver, the prices of all other minerals have significantly increased. The market price of gold bullion has been fluctuating. It fell for the three decades since 1980, increased in 2010, and began to decrease significantly in 2011. Due to both scarcity and high global demand, including strong demand in China, it is thus reasonable to presume strong inflationary effects in raw material markets.

Major items in the nonmetallic category are: antimony, cement, cobalt, industrial diamond, graphite, nitrogen, phosphate, potash, salt, and sulfur. However, average prices of the selected nonmetalic minerals are available from only 2010 in U.S.-producer price or average annual dealer prices.

7.4 RARE EARTH MINERALS

This section focuses on rare earth minerals (REMs). Most of them are materials essential for production of sophisticated military weapons and high technology items.

There are seventeen rare earth minerals, include helium-3, itrium, and dysprosium. Neodymium oxide is used in hard drives and magnets, and helium-3 is used for nuclear fusion. It is known that many REMs are essential for making military weapons such as lasers, smart bombs, guided missiles and night-vision goggles and also to make high-technol-

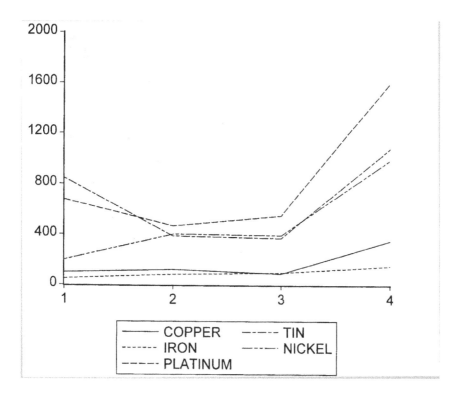

Figure 7.1. Average Prices of Major Minerals: 1980 (1) - 2010 (4). Note: 1 = 1980, 2 = 1990, 3 = 2000, 4 = 2010. Data: U.S. Census Bureau, Statistical Abstract of the United States: 2003, Washington, D.C.: U.S. GPO, p. 566 and ibid, 2012, p. 484 and p. 573.

ogy products such as the next generation of hybrid electric vehicles and wind turbines for jet engines. Therefore, REMs are serious resources of interest among superpowers and many industrial countries for their military expansions, especially during the period of political unrest in the world.

At present, the international REM market is controlled by China. China supplies 97 percent of the world's rare earth minerals to the market, which draws serious concern from other countries, including the United States. China has more than 50 percent of the REMs. In 2010, China temporarily halted the export of these minerals to Japan after diplomatic disputes between the two countries. Since then, the REM issue has become increasingly sensitive. The United States, EU and Japan have jointly asked the WTO for action in this matter. China states that it is in favor of effective management in accordance with WTO regulations but asks other countries to develop their own resources to share the burden of the global REM supply. According to the *Financial Times* (March 14, 2012, p.

2), major REM reserve countries are China (57.7 percent), Russia (3.6 percent), United States (9.1 percent), Australia (3.8 percent), and others that include Brazil, India, and Malaysia (15.8 percent).

From a geoeconomic standpoint, the REM market is important. Further research has to be done in this area.

7.5 MARITIME RESOURCES AND EXCLUSIVE ECONOMIC ZONES

As natural resources and energy available on land are limited and become scarcer, many industrial countries have begun to turn the sea and even outer space in pursuit of potential resources. Given the conflicts between countries over marine areas, it was necessary for the United Nations to reconcile maritime issues outside national territorial limits. An exclusive economic zone (EEZ) for a country is a maritime province over which the country has exclusive rights to explore and use marine resources, subject to international provisions. Article 55 in Part V of the Third United Nations Convention on the Law of the Sea in 1982 specifies the legal regime of the Exclusive Economic Zone as an area beyond and adjacent to the territorial sea. The rights and jurisdiction of the coastal state and the rights and freedoms of other states are governed by the relevant provisions of the Convention. There are two different kinds of maritime zones beyond the territorial waters restricted to twelve nautical miles from the coast or the baseline, "Contiguous zone of twelve nautical miles from the seaward edge of the territorial waters and the EEZ of 200 nautical miles from the base line." In terms of size of the EEZ, the countries selected here from among 197 are: United States ($11,351,000$ km^2), France ($11,935,000$), Australia ($8,505,348$), Russia ($8,505,348$), United Kingdom ($6,805,586$), New Zealand ($6,682,503$), Indonesia ($6,159,032$), Canada ($5,599,077$), Japan ($4,479,388$), and China ($3,879,666$).[10]

Except for a few countries, superpowers or countries surrounded by sea dominate this list. However, note that the maritime province for a country is not proportional to the size of the country's territory. Germany and Italy are not included in the above list. Their maritime provinces are not significant. In comparison to the actual country sizes, the maritime province of Russia is slightly larger than those of the U.K. and New Zealand; Canada' province is small and China has the smallest EEZ.

The EEZ may unnecessarily increase the possibility of future territorial disputes between any adjacent countries because it increases intersections of zones for mutual interests between/among contiguous countries. This possibility may lead to a conflict of economic interest that would lead to international political disputes and eventually to military confrontations in the future.

To understand how complex a territorial dispute can be, we consider an example in East Asia. Even without territorial intersections between countries in the absence of the EEZ, Korea and Japan have actually been in territorial disputes involving Dokdo (Takeshima), two small uninhabited rock isles in the East Sea (Sea of Japan) for several decades.[11] Chapter II Territory, Article 2 (a) of the San Francisco Peace Treaty, signed by forty-eight Allies and Japan in September 9, 1951, mandated that "Japan recognizing the independence of Korea, renounces all right, title and claim to Korea, including the islands of Quelpart, Port Hamilton and Dagelet."[12] Of course, the number of islands in this provision is not exhaustive. There are thousands of islands, large and small, that belong to Korea around its peninsula. As shown in numerous ancient maps, even maps published during Japanese colonial times (1910–1945), Dokdo was presented as part of Korean territory. Since the end of World War II, Korea has effectively ruled Dokdo for a period of over half a century. The twin isles are located in the East Sea (Sea of Japan) side by side, roughly sixty miles to the east of Ulleungdo (Port Hamilton) of three provincial counties with a population of over ten thousand. Korea has consistently maintained its official position that Dokdo is *historically* (as shown in numerous ancient documents and maps), *geographically* (by an actual distance of about 50–60 miles from mainland Korea) and *legally* (in terms of effective Korean rule for over fifty years in accordance with international laws) part of sovereign Korean territory.[13] Japan claims sovereignty on Dokto. Reportedly, Japan has not fully released their top secret documents on Dokdo that presumably argue against their claims. There was a time period of the "Japanese Expansion" (1898–1942) defined by historians.[14] This particular period, the period of Japanese imperialism, is an important criterion for clarifying these disputes. Would the Japanese claims of Dokdo be valid prior to this period? This question asks about the history and the length of history in connection with Dokdo that ascertain whether Japan would politicize its current disputes and revive its earlier colonialism in the twenty-first century. China has a similar issue with Japan in connection with Daoidau (Senkaku) in the East China Sea. In turn, China claims several other islands in the South China Sea as part of the lost territories in disputes with Japan, the Philippines, and Vietnam.

Under the regime of EEZ, there have already been numerous disputes between countries about territory, ecology, fisheries, and, most of all, oil reserves. Conflicts include the cases between the U.K and Iceland, Norway, and Russia; several neighboring countries in the South China Sea; Turkey and Greece, Italy, Slovenia, and Croatia in the Adriatic Sea; Canada and the United States; and France and Canada. Japan claims a vast EEZ as large as twenty-five times the land territory in the southwest Pacific Ocean, where there are so many tiny rock isles in the Okinawa area, including the Senkaku Isles allegedly secured as a similar form of EEZ in 1895 but in dispute with China at present. Japan is working hard to build underwater structures around the small rock isles to solidify the claims on them in the future.

Many industrialized countries are desperately seeking alternative energy sources and any minerals related to future energy needs, especially rare earth minerals, manganese and methane-hydrate. Most countries believe that resources and energy will eventually be depleted and want to maximize their territorial claims. Disputes and competition among countries over the EEZ are expected to increase in the future.

NOTES

1. Historians suggest that other contributing factors to the industrial revolutions are: (1) absence of internal and external barriers (such as taxes and tariffs) to trade, (2) early disappearance of serfdom, and (3) development of navigable rivers and canals.

2. See Chung, Jae Wan, *Utility and Production Functions: Theory and Applications,* Cambridge, Massachusetts: Blackwell, 1994, pp.147–51.

3. Professor Leontief's table is based on the formal definition of final demand that is the difference between total output and total input in each industrial sector, where the total input is proportional to the total output. The final demand in the expenditure standpoint is equivalent to the value-added in the distribution standpoint, i.e., $(I-A)Q = D$, where I = nxn identity matrix, A = nxn input-coefficient matrix, Q = a column vector of n number of outputs, D = a column vector of. n number of final demand. The output to meet the final demand is: $Q = (I-A)^{-1} D$.

4. See Chung (1994) who discusses both the Shephard duality theory and the Shephard lemma.

5. For references on earlier research in this area, see Eckstein and Wyss (1968) and Chung (1979) who used a generalized CES production function incorporated with the inter-industry flows of material inputs. Chung confirmed the significance of material costs in prices of finished goods. Contrary to the assumption imposed on constant costs of raw materials, changes in prices of raw materials are very sensitive to producers and their cost effects on the price of a finished good. The inflationary effects are quite significant.

6. See Kunzig (2011). In his article published recently in *Smithsonian* magazine, Graham Turner (1972), aresearcher at an MIT institute, predicted global economic collapse by 2030 and precipitous decline in population if the world's resources are consumed at the current pace, on the basis of the results obtained from the computer simulation. He also suggests that the world is on the track of disaster but green technologies for unlimited growth in his article, "Limited Growth."

7. See endnote 2 of chapter 1.

8. See the *Wall Street Journal,* September 11, 2014, p. A1 and p. A10.

9. U.S. producer price for copper (cents per lb.); average annual dealer price for platinum (dol./troy oz); average annual dealer price for gold and silver (99.95 percent purity); nationwide delivered basis for lead (cents per lb.); composite price for nickel and tin (cents/per lb.); Platt's Metals Week price for zinc (cents/per lb.); producer price index based on selling price for iron ore (1982=100). Data for nickel and iron ore in 1980 are unavailable. For the graphical purpose (figure 7.1), proxy numbers were used: 200 for ickel and 50 for iron ore.

10. The EEZ is not the same as the areas established to protect oceanic environment around small islands, exemplified by the U.S. Marine National Monuments in the Pacific Ocean, presumably on behalf of environmentalists.

11. See *Oxford Essential World Atlas,* Oxford University Press, 2011, p. 33.

12. The three islands are Jeju-do, Ulleung-do and Geomun-do, respectively, in Korean.

13. North Korea has no reason to disagree with South Korea on this issue.

14. See Roberts, J. M., *The New History of the World*, Oxford: Oxford University Press, 2002, p. 847. Note that Japan took Taiwan a little earlier in 1895 after Sino-Japan War.

EIGHT

Energy

Prior to the oil crisis in 1974, no one in oil consuming nations realized the economic importance of energy. Amid the abundance of cheap oil, there was no serious concern about the global oil market. Oil was little more than a standard commodity and was treated with indifference until the oil crises occurred in the 1970s. The repercussions of these oil crises on the world economy would prove to be enormous. After the detrimental effects of the first crisis, along with a long-term global economic stagnation over three decades, the international economy *per se* has become restructured as it has gravitated to a post-crisis equilibrium. Despite world-scale efforts for energy conservation and the development of alternative energy sources, however, there appear to be clear limits to reducing energy consumption in all oil-consuming nations. Furthermore, post-crisis technologies, in both production and consumption, have increasingly become more energy dependent. Conflicts of interest between oil-producing and oil-consuming countries (GED) are major observed phenomena since the oil crises of the 1970s (GHE).

Within the context of economics, energy is regarded as essential for both consumption and production. As a popular subject for economists, research on the demand for oil or energy in general has been widely performed. Price and income elasticities of demand for energy, (the Allen-Uzawa partial) elasticities of substitution between any pair of inputs to producers, and their policy implications have been the main objective.[1] Unlike the demand side, however, the supply of energy is interdisciplinary, requiring researchers to conduct geoeconomic studies.

There are renewable energy sources (hydro, nuclear, solar, tide, and wind) and nonrenewable energy sources (oil, natural gas and coal). Although nonrenewable sources are abundant and dominant for now, they are unquestionably finite and ultimately exhaustible.

113

This chapter focuses on fossil fuels—oil and natural gas—and nuclear energy and deals with the rest of the energy sources. All of the others, such as coal, hydro, solar, and wind, including future energy, are summarized briefly at the end the chapter.

At present, the global energy market is in a serious disparity in the global energy market:

(1) The United States has emerged as the biggest natural gas producer and one of the largest oil producers in the world. The energy-price equalization may appear to be a valid proposition.

(2) Global oil price has tumbled (from a range of 110 dollars per barrel to 80 dollars). Amid speculations on the crisis of the Russian economy in a floating situation, the world community is scared at the specter of World War III in connection with the conflict in Ukraine.[2]

These factors have amplified the significance of geoeconomic perspectives (see 8.7).

8.1 THE OIL CRISES IN THE 1970S

The oil crises of the 1970s marked a big turning point in not only the U.S. economy but also the world economy. The impact of the first oil crisis in 1974 on the global economy was especially huge. As the biggest oil consuming nation, the United States was most heavily affected. The direct cause of the crisis in 1974 was U.S. support of Israel in the Yom Kippur War with Egypt. Unlike the political motives of this crisis, the second oil crisis in 1978 was caused by massive economic pressure on the global oil market from the convergence of excess demand in each of the oil-consuming nations.

The U.S. economy was prosperous during the post–World War II period (1950s–early 1970s) but then began to decline rapidly and has remained in a long stagnation since the first oil crisis. Prior to the crisis, the price of oil was in the area of thirty cents per gallon; it is now in the range of three to four dollars in the United States. Figure 8.1 shows the average prices of fuels after 1980. Except for coal, prices of fossil fuels such as crude petroleum and natural gas have steadily increased since 1990. The average price of crude petroleum was twenty-two dollars per barrel in 1980 and rose to seventy-five dollars by the end of 2010. The price of natural gas remained stable at a low level until 1990 and continued to increase at steady rates in two stages, initially at a fast rate until 2000, followed by a moderate rate until 2010. The price of coal remained stable for about two decades since 1980 and then increased rapidly since 2000.

There have been various federal and local measures to reduce oil consumption. Efforts for energy conservation have continued for four decades. The Department of Energy was established in 1977 in pursuit of

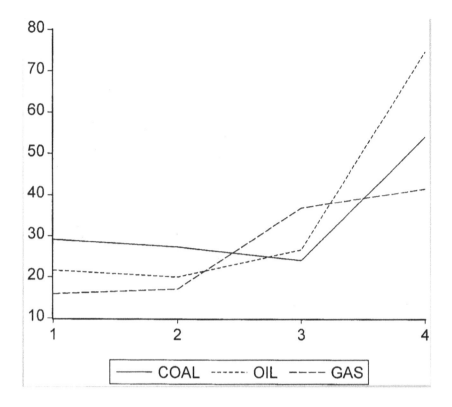

Figure 8.1. Average Prices of Mineral Fuels in the United States: 1980 (1) - 2010 (4). Note: Nationwide delivery price in the U.S., Years 1, 2, 3, and 4 are 1980, 1990, 2000, and 2010, respectively. The figure for bituminous coal in 2010 is not available. The figure for 2009 has been used instead as an approximation. Data: U.S. Census Bureau, Statistical Abstract of the United States, 2003, Washington, D.C.: U.S. GPO, p. 566 and 2012, p. 573.

effective energy policies. Most importantly, U.S. consumers began to realize the lasting importance of fuel efficiency. It was around this time that consumers began to embrace smaller, more fuel-efficient cars made by Japanese manufacturers such as Toyota and Honda. The cost of switching from the American auto industry, aggravated by labor disputes, was enormous. The big-three auto companies that once symbolized the might of American industry became two, despite receiving federal loans (except for Ford).

The adverse effects of the oil crises on the economies of other oil-consuming nations have been equally serious. Both industrialized and emerging countries have experienced situations similar to that of the United States. The high price of oil resulted in high inflation and unemployment in oil consuming nations. Given limited amounts of available oil and natural gas and their irregular supplies, the world economy has become unsustainable without conservation and alternative energy in addition to the need for stable energy supply and prices. Direct and indirect effects of the 1970s oil crises were in global economic downturns for several decades, except in a few newly industrialized countries in Asia. Clearly, chronic excess demand for energy without an adequate clearing mechanism is an important cause of global economic disparity (GED). This is not to criticize OPEC or oil-consuming nations but to attribute the primary cause of the crises to market failure in the global oil market.

Unlike during the period of cheap oil prior to the first oil crisis in 1974, energy has become a critical determining factor for activities of production and consumption. Both activities have increasingly become energy intensive, primarily because various technologies associated with them require producers and consumers to depend on more energy. Given the sparse endowments of oil across the globe, excess demand for oil at a high price in oil-consuming nations is expected to eventually lead to a new global oil crisis in the future. The current situation therefore requires the development of major alternative energy sources.

Finally, energy sources from fossil fuels have become magnified as economy-wide issues today, along with global warming driven in part by the burning of fossil fuels. This is a serious political and economic agenda today. Economic and political measures relating to oil markets are often interactive. Economic measures on the demand side taken by an oil consuming country, followed by retaliatory political measures on the supply side taken by OPEC, signify geoeconomic political impacts on energy-producing superpowers: (1) Saudi Arabia and other OPEC member countries, Russia, and the United States for crude petroleum; (2) Canada, Russia, Saudi Arabia and the United States for natural gas, both dry and liquid; (3) China, India and the United States for bituminous coal.

8.2 RESERVES, PRODUCTION, AND CONSUMPTION OF ENERGY IN THE WORLD

Figure 8.2 provides information on world oil resources (proved resources) available in OPEC and non-OPEC countries for 1995–2025. Their portions are 56 percent and 44 percent of the total resource, respectively. Oil resources are also broken down further by country and region. The main ones are Africa, Canada, China, the Middle East, Mexico, Russia, South America and the United States. Figure 8.3 shows their resources. Observe the tallest bar in the middle of the figure for the Middle East as of 2005. Like raw materials, oil resources are not evenly distributed across the world. There are serious conflicts of interest between producing and consuming countries, and thus chances for market failure are high.

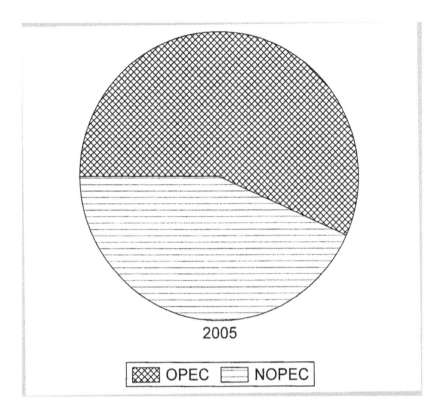

2005

OPEC   NOPEC

Figure 8.2. World Oil Reserves: OPEC and Non-OPEC. Note: 1995-2025, in billion barrels. Numbers for oil reserves are sum of proved reserves, reserve growth, undiscovered. Data: U.S. Energy Information Administration, International Energy Outlook, Washington, D.C.: U.S. GPO, December 2005, p. 6.

Energy-consuming regions and/or countries are also responsible for shortages of energy as well as environmental problems in the world and thus ultimately for GED. Figure 8.4 is concerned with energy production (not reserves) by region and type of energy. As of 2008, Asia and Oceania (136.3.quadrillion BTUs), North America (101.7), Eurasia (71.7) and the Middle East (68.2) are big producers in the world. The total energy production in the same year (491.4) consists of oil (166.0 quadrillion BTUs), coal (142.0) and natural gas (113.2). The first two regions and Europe are the biggest consumers.

By country, Iran, Saudi Arabia, and other OPEC members, the United States and Russia are the major crude oil–producing countries. The major energy-consuming countries are mostly industrialized and emerging countries. They are the United States, Brazil, Canada, China, France, Germany, India, Italy, Japan, South Korea, Mexico, Russia, and the U.K.

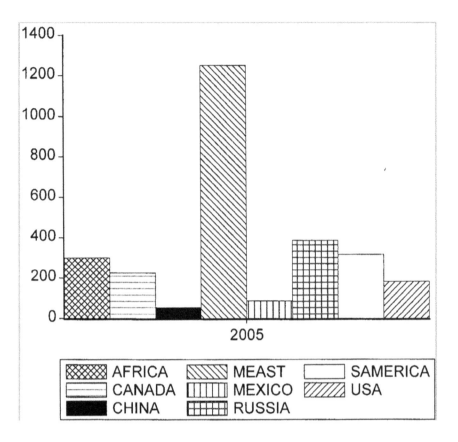

Figure 8.3.   Estimated World Oil Reserves (1995-2025; billion barrels). Data: U.S.
Energy Information Administration, International Energy Outlook, Washington,
D.C.: U.S. GPO, December 2005, p. 6.

(1) Asia and the Pacific region consume more energy (oil, coal, natural gas, and nuclear energy) than they produce. Japan, South Korea, and other rapidly developing countries consume more than they produce. China consumes and produces a lot but in almost the same amounts.

(2) Consumption by Western Europe exceeds its production. Europe and Eurasia consume slightly more natural gas than oil.

(3) North America consumes more than it produces in the order of oil, gas, and coal.

As a result, imported crude oil prices get higher.

8.3 OIL

Among the various energy sources, oil is the main source. This section focuses on global oil markets.

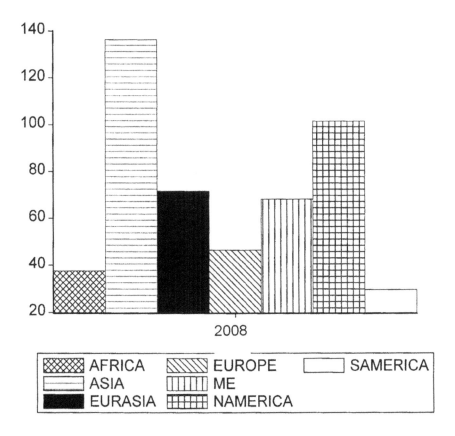

Figure 8.4. World Primary Energy Production by Region (in quadrillion BTU).
Note: Figure for Africa in 2007. Data: U.S. Census Bureau, Statistical Abstract of
the United States: 2012, Washington, D.C.: U.S. GPO, p. 863.

8.3.1. Oil Reserves

The quantity of oil existing in this planet should be enormous. However, no one knows the exact amount. Only a fraction of the subsurface
reservoir, that is, oil in place, can be recovered and is referred to as the
"producible reserve," which can be broken down into proven reserves
and unproven reserves.[3] Although economists do not need to know
about technical aspects of oil in detail, it is helpful to outline the metho-
dology followed by geological specialists in this area. They suggest a
number of methods of calculating proven and unproven reserves. In addition, the quality of oil varies. There is light and heavy oil and oil mixed
with impure contents like sulfur or sand. For example, most oil reserves
in Venezuela are extra-heavy petroleum with high amounts of sulfur.
Given the uncertainty involved in defining oil with various physical
characteristics and extraction technologies, readers should keep in mind

that the data presented in this chapter, much of which is compiled from different sources, are intended to provide only a rough guide. Consequently, the figures in each table are not necessarily exact and consistent throughout. They should be approximated at the reader's discretion.

By definition, an oil reserve is the producible fraction of oil in place. Actual production of oil is, in general, proportional to the total oil reserves. In the case of an OPEC nation, production is subject to change in international demand and oil revenue in GNP; it is also proportional to the quota set by OPEC. The amount of total reserves in the world is reportedly over 1 trillion barrels as of 2011. Venezuela, Saudi Arabia, Canada, and Iran hold 60 percent of world oil reserves.[4]

8.3.2 Supply of Oil

The supply side of oil relates to complex intra-country politics and inter-country geoeconomic implications. Over the three decades since 1980, the U.S. House of Representatives has been in favor of new drilling. However, the executive branch has consistently been against it for various reasons. For example, the House passed a bill for drilling in the Arctic National Wildlife Refuge. But President Clinton vetoed it. There have also been bills for offshore oil and gas drilling.[5] However, the White House has consistently been against new drilling, and the Senate has rejected such bills on the grounds of safety issues in environmentally sensitive areas. Instead, the current administration focuses on extensions of existing leases and lease sales, case by case, for a limited period such as one year (extended up to ten years, subject to new safety requirements), coordinated by an interagency task force. These areas include the western and central Gulf of Mexico. They are subject to a temporary moratorium on drilling imposed against British Petroleum since its 2010 oil spill. In the Alaskan slopes, the Shell Oil Company plans have been delayed by an air pollution permit. The lease sale for the Virginia coast is expected to be on the agenda in 2017 at the earliest. The underlying economic and political rationales are eliminating taxpayer subsidies to oil and gas companies and creating jobs. As gasoline prices increased to about four dollars per gallon (as of May 2011) in many parts of the country, both the legislative and the executive branches moved to expedite the supply of oil and gas to stabilize the domestic prices.[6] From the inter-country political perspective, the supply of oil and natural gas by the United States has an important geoeconomic implication in connection with the EU's dependence on Russian energy sources

There are two different entities that harness the supply of oil to world markets. They are OPEC and non-OPEC countries:

(A) OPEC

OPEC (Organization of Petroleum Exporting Countries) was created by five countries (Iran, Iraq, Kuwait, Saudi Arabia, and Venezuela) in 1960, based on a proposal by Venezuela along with Iran, and joined later by nine other countries. At present, there are twelve member countries (five founding member countries plus Algeria, Angola, Ecuador, Libya, Nigeria, Qatar, and the United Arab Emirates). Its headquarters was in Geneva for the first five years and has now been in Vienna, Austria, since 1965. Among the twelve members, Saudi Arabia, Iran, Iraq, Kuwait, the UAE, and Venezuela are the six countries that have most of the oil reserves in OPEC and, as of 2010, produce slightly above 40 percent of the oil for all consuming nations in the world.

The purpose of OPEC is to safeguard members' interests by stabilizing prices in international oil markets, securing a steady income to member countries, providing an efficient and regular supply of oil to consuming nations, and ensuring a fair return on investment in the petroleum industry. However, OPEC has been criticized because of its behavior as an oil cartel that allocates output rationing to member countries to fix prices, adjusted not necessarily by economic rationales but by a member's political circumstances. At the time of the first oil crisis in 1973, the embargo by some OPEC countries against Western countries supporting Israel in the Yom Kippur War increased the price of crude oil by four times, followed by a 10 percent increase in January 1975, and another oil crisis in 1978.

(B) Non-OPEC Oil Producing Countries

Major non-OPEC countries include Canada, Mexico, Russia, the U.K. and the United States. They produce 56 percent of the oil (see figure 8.2). Russia alone accounts for 14.8 percent of total world oil production. Brent crude oil is produced in the North Atlantic basin by Shell UK Exploration and Production on behalf of Exxon Mobile and Royal Dutch Shell. As the leading price benchmark for Atlantic basin crude oil, it is used to price two-thirds of traded crude oil.

Overall, the capacity and production of OPEC with respect to non-OPEC producers and to the world total are large enough to suggest that OPEC's influence on the world oil market is enormous, which has generated lasting effects on the global economy. The economies of OPEC member countries are heavily reliant on their exports of oil. In Saudi Arabia, oil accounts for 90 percent of exports and 55 percent of GDP.[7] In Venezuela, oil accounts for 95 percent of exports and 12 percent of GDP.[8]

8.3.3 Demand for Oil

Unlike the supply side, the demand side of oil is a key area for analysis oriented toward economics. Although countless studies have been done on both the behavior of households and firms since the 1930s, research on the demand for energy/oil by households or firms was extensively conducted during the post–oil crisis period. There are two different kinds of oil consumption, household demand and industrial demand. Three discrete economic research models on the demand side are: validity of the law of demand for energy/oil, effects of energy cost on inflation, and substitutability between energy and other productive factors. Economists confirm the significant impact of the 1970s oil crises on the U.S. national as well as the global economy. A majority of economists agree that a higher price for gasoline reduces its demand and results in substitution among productive factors. In response to subsequent inflationary effects, consumers switch transportation modes.[9]

The United States obtains oil from over thirty-five countries, including, in order, the top three exporters: Canada, Mexico, and Saudi Arabia. This diversity makes supplies more secure for the United States, implying that many different producers are competing for access to the American market. In 2006,

- The United States produced one-third of the oil, and
- Canada and Mexico supplied approximately 20 percent; thus, two-thirds of U.S. oil consumed was produced in North and South America.
- Oil-producing countries in the Middle East supply 15 percent.
- Countries in Africa emerging as major suppliers to the United States supply about 15 percent.[10]

8.3.4 Prices of Oil in the World Market

It is a fundamental proposition in economics that the equilibrium price of a particular commodity, including oil, is competitively determined by its supply and demand in the corresponding market. However, in the case of oil-producing countries in the Middle East and others, OPEC members (41 percent of market share in 2010) or not, producers are state-monopoly agents. In the absence of a competitive supply of oil, oil-producing countries are likely subject more to global geoeconomics. Oil-consuming countries are virtually price-takers.

The world's supply and demand increased from approximately eighty million barrels per day in 2003 to about ninety million barrels per day in 2010, and these levels are expected to exceed one-hundred million barrels per day by 2020. The price of oil has always been a primary concern for both consuming and producing nations. To consuming nations, a high price is inflationary and recessionary. To producing countries, a high price increases oil revenue, which changes the international financial structure in their favor. In principle, there are a few reasons for the high price of oil in the world:

1. Strong demand for oil by emerging Asian countries, including China and India, due to their rapid economic growth, and a revived U.S. demand for oil in the recent past. [11]
2. Irregularity in production due to political unrest in major oil-producing countries.
3. Considering the recent global financial crisis and long-term stagnation at present, however, the rate of increase may be sluggish.

The global oil price has radically fluctuated, as compiled below:

> The price of crude oil rose from 30 dollars per barrel in 1973 to 140.97 dollars as of July 2, 2008, a record level. [12] Brent crude oil price nose-dived to 44 dollars in 2010, rose as high as about 110 dollars for 2011–2014, dropped sharply to 70.15 dollars and further to 66.15 dollars as of November 28, 2014, and is expected to be 45 dollars in 2030.

Since the oil crisis in 1973, the average price of oil has stayed high with some minor fluctuations. However, oil prices have kept dropping sharply over the past three months before plummeting in November 2014. OPEC failed to agree to deal with the delicate situation generated by U.S. shale oil of approximately four million barrels per day supplied to the global oil market of seventy-five million barrels since 2008 and expected to be supplied at a profitable price estimated above forty-two dollars.

The underlying rationale for the price of oil is a simple economic principle for equilibrium price as determined by the laws of supply and demand. Excess demand/supply results in an increase/decrease of the price. With oil, however, its supply is often tied to geoeconomic politics among OPEC members (yielding intermittent production quotas that result in radical price fluctuations) and major non-OPEC countries.

If the price of oil increases, the general price index jumps up. Extensive research on the correlation between oil price and the general price index was done during the years following the 1970s oil crises. [13] The IMF warned that the rise in oil along with food prices could seriously damage the economies of developing countries. [14] According to the International Energy Agency (IEA) in Paris, the increase in the world's need for energy caused by industrialization and population growth is expected to be 51 percent by 2030. The IEA predicted that global oil markets will remain tight during the next five years.

It is expected that OPEC's ability to control the price of oil in the world market will diminish in the future as oil-consuming countries start to develop their oil reserves. In addition to shale oil produced in North Dakota and Texas, reserves in Alaska, the North Sea, the East Coast (Virginia), and the Gulf of Mexico are huge. The United States has emerged as a major energy producer. Industrial demand for oil has recently decreased significantly. However, the price of oil would not significantly decrease because of continuing strong demand for oil by developing countries including China. The chronic world shortage of oil and the global environmental problems caused by burning fossil fuels require each country to focus on developing new technologies for alternative energy. The need to explore alternative sources necessarily rises as the price of oil increases.

There is one underlying mechanism in the global oil markets for determining the equilibrium price of oil, at least for large consuming nations. The diversification of exporting sources by oil importing countries would help to enhance competition among major oil exporting countries.

8.4 NATURAL GAS

Unlike the case of oil and coal, almost all regions around the world have natural gas, endowed with the heavy concentrations in the Middle East, Europe, and Russia. In the Middle East, Iran and Qatar hold approximately 50 of 70 billion tons of oil equivalent (BtOe) of reserves in the region. As of 2005, Russia has the largest amount of reserves in the world. It holds about 55 of 68 BtOe of reserves, equivalent to about 35 percent of natural gas *reserves* in the world. As exhibited in figure 8.5, Russia, Iran, and Qatar have about 75 percent of the world's total of natural gas reserves. Figure 8.6 is concerned with gas *production* by country. The United States and Russia are two major production countries. They produce almost the same amount, 20.96 and 20.61 trillion cubic feet, respectively, in 2009. In that year, the world total was 106.47. In his 2012 State of the Union Address, President Obama announced that the United States had enough natural gas reserves for 100 years.

Finally, it is known that Russia is the country of the largest natural gas reserves (approximately 1/3 percent) as well as production (1/5 percent) in the world and has the eighth largest oil reserves and the largest production among the non-OPEC countries. Natural gas is the top energy item exported by Russia, mostly to Europe. Russia supplies natural gas and oil to Europe through massive pipelines.[15] Both natural gas and oil supplied by Russia to Europe have often been a serious geoeconomic issue. Steady decreases in oil prices in the international oil market at present are serious concerns of Russia and OPEC. For the history on energy geoeconomics, see section 8.7 for details.

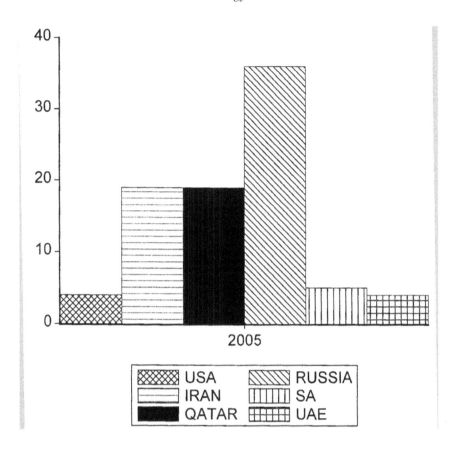

Figure 8.5. Natural Gas Reserves in the World (percent, June 2005). Data: U.S. Energy Information Administration, International Energy Outlook, Washington, D.C.: U.S. GPO, 2007. Data rearranged by author.

8.5 NUCLEAR ENERGY

Global shortages of oil and natural gas have forced countries to depend on nuclear energy. There has been a series of arguments against fossil fuel consumption, such as the irregular supply of oil, steady increases in the price of oil, dependence on foreign oil, and environmental problems (i.e., greenhouse gases that trap heat in the earth's atmosphere), all of which have motivated countries to develop alternative energy sources. Nuclear energy initially emerged as a relatively clean and economical source. However, a series of the disasters, at Three Mile Island in 1979, Chernobyl in 1986, and Fukushima in 2011, was and still is serious enough to warn the entire world against total dependence on nuclear energy. Despite grave concerns about radioactivity released from these successive disasters (which may remain on earth for a million years), the

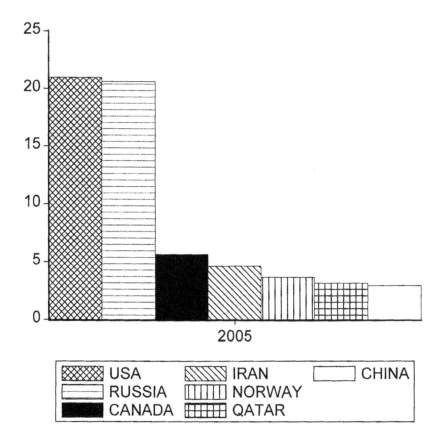

Figure 8.6. Natural Gas Production by Country (2009, in trillion cubic feet). Data: U.S. Census Bureau, Statistical Abstract of the United States: 2012, Washington, D.C., U.S. GPO, p. 865.

popularity of nuclear energy remained in industrialized countries (except Germany) in the early 1990s for economic reasons. However, Germany has decided to shut down all nuclear facilities by 2025. The shares of renewable energy from sun, wind, and biomass are expected to rise to 80 percent of electricity production and 60 percent of overall energy use by 2050. Japan decided to follow the German nuclear-policy plan after the Fukushima disaster in 2011 and considers geothermal sources for alternative energy. These decisions appear to be politicized and thus remain to be seen for the future.

As of 2010, there are 441 nuclear reactors in the world; these reactors operate in thirty-two countries, and they provide 16 percent of the electricity produced in the world. The number of reactors under construction is twenty-nine in India, Russia, and China. Over the next three decades,

Table 8.1.   Commercial Nuclear Reactors by Country: 2010

Country	Number of Reactors In Operation	Electricity produced (bil. Kwh)	Percentage of World Total
(1) 11 Major Countries in Terms of Number of Reactors in Operation			
U.S.	104	864.1 (19.3 percent)	31.0
France	58	52.2 (78.5)	16.1
Japan	54	292.3 (29.3)	9.4
Russia	32	167.8 (15.8)	5.9
Korea, R.	20	149.7 (44.7)	5.5
U.K.	19	NA (19.9)	
Canada	19	52.2 (14.6)	3.4
Germany	17	140.5	5.4
Ukraine	15	69.1	3.2
China	13	NA	2.5
Sweden	10	58.2	2.3
(2) 21 other countries	132		
32 countries	29[a]	(16.0)	
13 countries			

Note:
   NA = Not available.
   [a] The number of reactors under construction.
   Sources:
   1. U.S. Census Bureau, *Statistical Abstract of the United States*: 2010, p. 866. Platts Energy, A Division of the McGraw-Hill Companies, Inc.
   2. International Atomic Energy Agency, reported by *Washington Post*, January 6, 2007, Saturday, A1 and A14.

the United States, the EU other than Germany, and countries in the Persian Gulf have plans to build about 100 reactors. For details, see table 8.2.

Here is some fragmentary information on nuclear energy summarized as follows:

Table 8.2.   Commercial Nuclear Reactors by Country: 2010

Country	Number of Reactors In Operation	Electricity produced (bil. Kwh)	Percentage of World Total
(1) 11 Major Countries in Terms of Number of Reactors in Operation			
U.S.	104	864.1 (19.3 percent)	31.0
France	58	52.2 (78.5)	16.1
Japan	54	292.3 (29.3)	9.4
Russia	32	167.8 (15.8)	5.9
Korea, R.	20	149.7 (44.7)	5.5
U.K.	19	NA (19.9)	
Canada	19	52.2 (14.6)	3.4
Germany	17	140.5	5.4
Ukraine	15	69.1	3.2
China	13	NA	2.5
Sweden	10	58.2	2.3
(2) 21 other countries	132		
32 countries	29a		
13 countries		(16.0)	

Note:

NA = Not available.

Source: http://en/wikipedia.org/wiki/Energy in Russia pp. 2-3ª The number of reactors under construction.

Sources:

(1) U.S. Census Bureau, *Statistical Abstract of the United States*: 2010, p. 866. Platts Energy, A Division of the McGraw-Hill Companies, Inc.

(2) International Atomic Energy Agency, reported by *Washington Post*, January 6, 2007, Saturday, A1 and A14.

1. As of 2008, the ten major producers in terms of percentage of global total are:
2. United States (31.0 percent), France (16.1), Japan (9.4), Russia (5.9), South Korea (5.5), Germany (5.4), Canada (3.4), Ukraine (3.2), China (2.5) and Sweden (2.3).[16]

3. Russia is the fourth largest country of nuclear energy. Nonetheless, Russia has increased nuclear energy production, presumably to offset gas exported abroad. Note that Germany is taking the opposite course due to environmental concerns. Germany has a plan to shut down all of its 17 nuclear power plants by 2025.

4. Currently, 29 nuclear power plants are being built all over the world, including in China and India. China is among the top ten countries producing nuclear energy. Although its percentage figure is relatively small so far, China plans to build four additional plants. India is rushing to build seven more plants. The other countries are Japan (1), South Korea (1), Taiwan (2), Pakistan (1), Iran (1), Russia (5), Argentina (1), Bulgaria (2), Romania (1), Ukraine (2) and Finland (1).

5. Sweden and Norway are contiguous within the same region. It is interesting to observe that Sweden produces nuclear energy, whereas Norway relies on hydroelectricity.

The 2011 Fukushima disaster in Japan warned the world once again to reconsider nuclear energy as a power source. Despite the challenge of anticipated shortages of power in the future, Japan has decided to move toward zero nuclear power. All fifty-four nuclear reactors in Japan will be closed and about 30 percent of the electricity gleaned from nuclear power will be provided by other sources, such as thermo-power plants that are already over forty years old, geothermal plants in hot-spring areas, and wind-power plants in coastal areas. Japan will also try to reduce the consumption of energy in the household, manufacturing, and commercial sectors.

8.6 COAL, HYDROPOWER, SOLAR, WIND, AND BIOFUEL

Despite relatively small energy sources in comparison with oil and natural gas, coal and hydropower are traditional and reliable sources, solar and wind are insignificant and still in experimental stages but are natural and clean sources, and biofuel is a new and possible future source.

1. Coal was a dominant energy source and is still a significant source. Coal is relatively abundant around the world, with major concentrations in three different continents—Europe, Asia/Pacific, and North America: About 500 million tons of oil equivalent (MtOe) in Europe, 2,000 MtOe in Asia/Pacific, and 700 MtOe in North America. It is cheaper than oil. However, there is a global trend to ban coal in the future over environmental concerns.

2. Hydropower has been an important, conventional, and safe energy source. However, it requires a specific topographical feature. There are many countries that generate electricity by means of hydro-

power. Included are China (14.3 percent of the world total), Brazil (12.3), Canada (12.2), United States (8.3), Russia (5.8), Norway (4.4), India (4.1), Venezuela (2.8), Japan (2.4) and Sweden (2.2) as of 2008. The hydropower percentage of the world's total is only 6.3 percent. There are some countries that rely entirely on hydropower. Most of them are small nations in Africa.

3. Solar energy is available only on sunny days. It radiates back to space and is absorbed by gases in the atmosphere, warming up the earth. Contrary to common thought, generating energy by means of wind force is difficult and expensive.[17]

4. Biofuel emerges as a future energy source.[18] In 1985, the popular movie *Back to the Future* showed a time-traveling car powered by the fuel from ordinary household garbage. Even if this energy source came from the mind of a Hollywood writer, the interest is still there. Renewable energy has begun to grow a market. Global efforts for sustainable "going green" would hopefully protect the planet by harnessing technology to recycle waste and create cleaner energy to secure the clean environment for future generations.

8.7 GEOECONOMICAL INSIGHTS INTO ENERGY

The global energy market is heavily related to international economy and politics that have also intersections with the geographical domain in many ways. A country or a group of countries, either energy producing or consuming, strives to maximize its interest in the world energy market. This is where political and economic interests in energy-consuming nations are in conflict with energy-producing countries. Their geoeconomic games take place often with mutual international political leverages and policies.

Britain and France were the primary foreign players in the Middle East in the post–World War I era. Major U.S. interest in the Middle East, especially the Persian Gulf and Israel, began after World War II, under the overall directions of energy policies or perspectives in each administration, as outlined below:

- The State Department emphasized oil resources in the Middle East as a major source of strategic power in a memorandum to President Truman.
- President Eisenhower recognized the Middle East as the most strategically important region in the world.
- Henry Kissinger, the national security advisor to President Nixon, thought that higher price of energy would mainly affect Europe and Japan and improve U.S. competitiveness in the world market.[19]
- Zbigniew Brzezinski, the national security advisor to President Carter, viewed the relatively low costs of Middle Eastern oil as a

U.S. economic benefit and recognized the American security role in the Middle East as leverage on the European and Asian economies.

Some notable issues and problems emerged in the recent past are summarized as follows:

- The oil crisis in 1974, resulting from embargos imposed by OPEC against the United States, became a turning point of U.S. foreign policy toward the Middle East.
- There are standing issues and problems between Russia and the EU in connection with pipelines for oil and natural gas.
- The Gulf of Mexico disaster in 2011 was costly not only to British Petroleum but also the United States.
- A potential Arctic oil spill in the future is a scenario that reminds us to imagine an environmental disaster as a consequence of human recklessness.

There are also geoeconomic implications in distribution of energy. Energy is distributed all over the world mostly by marine transportation through many strategically sensitive spots in the world, including canals and straits. The Suez Canal, Panama Canal, Strait of Gibraltar, Strait of Hormuz, and Strait of Malacca are the main watchtowers for energy transportation today. Among them, the last two are good examples for the recent incidents:

1. The Strait of Hormuz, the narrow strait between the Persian Gulf and the Gulf of Oman (the world's most strategically important checkpoint, where a U.S. naval base is reportedly in Bahrain), is the primary route of oil exports from a region including the six OPEC member countries.[20] At present (since March 2012), there is a standoff between the United States and Iran due to the threat of a Hormuz blockade by Iran in response to U.S. warnings against Iranian nuclear testing.
2. The Strait of Malacca, the narrow stretch of water between the Malay peninsula of and Sumatra in Indonesia, is one of the most important shipping channels that link the Indian and Pacific Oceans. It is critically important for Far East economies such as those of China, Japan, and Korea. Between half a million and one million vessels pass through the strait in a year to transport about one-quarter of the world's traded goods, including oil. Imagine a scenario in which this passage is blocked due to critical differences in geoeconomic interests between any two countries, followed by a concurrent blockage of the South China Sea. Shipments of oil from the Middle East to the Far East would cease. Damage to the regional economy as well as the impact on the global economy are beyond the imagination.

We now turn to further insights into geoeconomic global energy (oil and natural gas) markets:

(1) Mutual interests, pressures, and tensions between oil-consuming and oil-producing countries have resulted in serious political as well as economic problems. Since the first oil crisis, a common objective of oil-consuming nations, amid their clamoring for energy primacy, has been to secure dependable supplies of oil and natural gas. In response to any economic or political action by one country against another, retaliatory economic or political counter-measures by the latter is initially the case, often followed by military threats or involvement. For example, manufacturing industries react to a geoeconomic conflict by pulling out of their investments in the inflicting country. Western investors actually pulled out of Russia during the crisis in Georgia in August 2008. Some economic researchers and energy agencies, such as the International Energy Agency (IEA), predict that global oil markets will remain tight for some time in the future. Contrary to such a tight situation, an adverse case like market oversupply could develop. In the 1980s, Iraq increased its oil production in a likely attempt to pay for the Iran-Iraq War. Unlike the expectations of Iraq, however, the increase in the supply of oil combined with a decrease in demand for oil in consuming nations resulted in excess supply, known as the 1980s oil gluts. Steady decreases in the price of oil for six years by 46 percent in 1986 significantly reduced total revenue. Demand for oil decreased due to energy conservation, development of alternative energy sources, and sufficient oil reserves built up by consuming countries since the time of the 1974 oil crisis. As a result, Iraq made the mistake of assuming that the demand for oil would always be inelastic. The six-year oil glut was followed by the Gulf War in 1990–1991, after which the price of oil fell to fifteen dollars per barrel in the late 1990s, and Iraq asked OPEC to push up oil prices. However, the OPEC countries at that time were divided by regional wars and disputes about production quotas. Saudi Arabia was against the policy of expensive oil and uneasy about uncertain supply in the future. In the current crisis, Saudi Arabia is cutting oil prices for Asia and the United States, a move that appears to begin competition for international market share.

(2) The Caspian Natural Gas Basin and Baku oil fields: The Caspian region consists of five littoral states, Russia, Iran, Azerbaijan, Kazakhstan, and Turkmenistan. The basin is rich in oil.[21] Baku is the center of the region's international oil industry. Trans-border pipelines in the Caspian region under the Caspian Pipeline Consortium Project (CPC) are connected with Russian pipelines linked as a cobweb leading toward Europe. The pipeline linking Baku (Azerbaijan), –Tbilisi (Georgia)–Ceyhan (Turkey) that flows Azerbaijan oil straight to a Mediterranean port and the pipelines between Baku–Tikhoretsk and Atyrau–Samara are also primary lines. However, Pkhrikian (2012) rejects some optimistic estimates that the Caspian oil reserves are about the same size as in the Persian Gulf's, and he states that some are exaggerated.[22]

Between Russia and Europe, there are two different kinds of pipelines, one for oil and the other for natural gas. Oil pipelines starting at the Timan–Pechora basin and the West Siberian basin in northern Russia spread out to Europe in all directions. Lines to St. Petersburg, Gdansk, Leipzig, Prague, Odessa, and several other places cover most of the European continent. The Yamal fields–Baumgarten (the gas hub in Germany) is a major gas line. There are also several oil and gas pipelines proposed for the future.[23]

(3) Countries with major reserves of natural gas are Russia, Iran, Qatar, Saudi Arabia, Nigeria, the United States, and Venezuela. Among them, Russia is the country with the largest reserves of gas. Europe imports 23 percent of its total natural gas consumption from Russia, which accounts for 60 percent of Russian gas exports. Gas flows from Russia to European countries such as Germany, Italy, France, Hungary, Poland, Austria, and Slovakia through countless pipelines, including a long pipeline in Slovakia, the main gateway for Russian gas to Europe. Russian gas pipelines to Europe look like a giant cobweb. Among the many pipelines, the line that links Russia and Central Asia via Kazakhstan has become controversial between Russia and the West at present. Contrary to the European preference for a pipeline under the Caspian Sea to Europe in order to diversify supply routes, this is a line that was built on Russian conditions to supply gas to Europe only through Russia. In addition, the North European gas pipeline construction under the Baltic Sea was negotiated favorably between Russia and Germany. At the German request for more gas supply, Russia agreed to supply 100 billion cubic meters to Germany over the ten years following November 15, 2006. This amount is equivalent to a maximum of 100 billion cubic meters of gas production by 2015; half of the maximum is required to be set aside for Russian domestic use. In order to accommodate the supply committed to Germany, Russia substituted central Asian gas for Russian supplies to the rest of the Commonwealth of Independent States. It was a period of recession in the United States, the longest downturn of the U.S. economy in a quarter century, followed by the global financial crisis. It appears that Russia might have foreseen the upcoming global financial crisis and was determined to secure Germany, the richest and largest energy consuming nation in Europe, as the country of choice to guarantee a long-term, uninterrupted demand. Supplies to Italy dropped by 25 percent and to France by 30 percent. Many central and eastern European countries dropped by even more. Despite the assurances of Gazprom, Russia's state-owned gas monopoly, for more gas to be exported to Europe, European countries became concerned about the risk of higher prices in the future, stemming from the gas politics. As the latest development in this area, there is also the Russia-China natural gas deal of 400 billion dollars for thirty years in May 2014. Of course, details on inter-country gas deals require bilateral contracts.

The pipelines branch out of Russia to numerous European countries, demonstrates the energy dependence of Europe on Russia and thus the chance for gas disputes between Russia and Europe at any time. A

Russia-Ukraine dispute over gas occurred on January 1, 2006. At that time Russia cut the gas flowing into a pipeline that crosses the Ukraine, a country in pursuit of political independence from Russia and moving toward the West; this, in turn, resulted in cutting the gas supply to Europe. The recent dramatic escalation of political and military tensions between Russia and Ukraine-United States in connection with Crimea incidents and Russia's increase of gas price against Ukraine are basically an issue over energy. Intra-European disputes among gas consuming nations are also likely in the future. Meanwhile, the United States began to negotiate with Kazakhstan to build a gas pipeline to Europe bypassing Russian territory, under the Caspian Sea and then through Azerbaijan, Georgia, and Turkey. Today, the pipeline from Baku to Ceyhan in Turkey serves as a diversified supply route to Europe.[24]

European dependence on Russian gas is a complex geoeconomic issue. In the short run, European countries need to coordinate their bargaining position and to deliberate alternative infrastructure such as marine terminals for delivery and storage of liquefied natural gas. Europe and Russia need to negotiate a long-term uninterrupted supply and demand to be ensured with prices adjusted by both sides. In the long run, however, only the economic principle for competition will bring about mutual satisfactions. In order to minimize risks for both, European countries need to diversify supply routes to other producing countries in the long run.

NOTES

1. See Chung (1987) and chapter 7 (7.1) of this book for details.
2. See *The Economist*, November 22, 2014.
3. Many countries keep strategic petroleum reserves controlled by their government for the purposes of economic and national security. The United States' reserves are reportedly 4.1 billion barrels, of which 1.4 billion gallons are controlled by the government.
4. See the data source for figure 8.2.
5. See the *Washington Post*, December 22, 2005, p. A10.
6. See Darlene Supperville and Dina Cappiello, AP, May 14, 2011.
7. See U.S. Energy Information Administration, *International Energy Outlook*, December 2005, p. 6. Also see U.S. Census Bureau, *Statistical Abstract of the United States*, 2012, p. 863.
8. http://www.state.gov/r/pa/ei/bn/35766.htm, accessed May 5, 2012, p. 6.
9. See Chung (1981), pp. 77–86.
10. Exxon Mobil in *Washington Post*, March 27, 2007, A17.
11. Economic growth is an important factor for a projection of changes in a country's or the world's future energy consumption.
12. The *Wall Street Journal*, p. A8 and p. C6.
13. See Chung (1987).
14. *Financial Times*, July 2, 2008, p. 11.
15. Readers of this book may imagine a giant cobweb for the massive Russian oil and gas pipelines.

16. Oxford, University Press, p. 25.

17. Ibid., p. 25.

18. Caroline Chung has suggested discussing biofuel briefly here as a forward-looking energy issue today.

19. http://www.politicalforum.com/terrorism/146055-us-imperial-planning-middle-east. . .,
accessed May 23, 2012.

20. The amount is approximately 20 percent of the world's oil, which is about 35 percent of seaborne trade. See U.S. Energy Information Administration, *World Oil Transit Checkpoints.*
http://www.eia.gov/countries/regions-topics.cfm?fips=WOTC#hormuz, Accessed January 14, 2012.

21. The oil reserve is reportedly almost equivalent to the size of annual U.S. GDP, 12 trillion dollars.

22. See Pkhrikian, Artashes, "Geopolitics of the Caspian Oil," at
http://www.vahan.com/armenianway/aw/Pkhrikian_Artashes/index.html, accessed April 30, 2012. He suggests that the Caspian region contains no more than two to three percent of the world's proven oil reserves and that its importance has been politicized by competition over oil pipelines.

23. Natural gas produced in Jamal peninsular is reportedly over 90 percent of the total amount of natural gas produced in Russia.

24. Russian Gazettes and the Russian News and Information Agency, "The Gas Race,"
Trend line Russia, U.S. edition, An Advertising Supplement to *The Washington Post,*
November 15, 2006, p. H3.

NINE

The Environment, Global Warming, and Water Resources

Planet earth is relentlessly affected by earthquakes, volcanic activities, ocean currents, hydrological cycles, hurricanes and tornadoes, and other natural environmental events. There is nothing that human beings can do directly to control vibrations from earthquakes, hot ash spewed by volcanic eruptions, hemispheric ocean currents, oscillatory patterns of temperature on the sea surface, storms or tornados where warm and cold air currents meet, and changes in seasons. However, a considerable part of environmental problems is attributed to manmade causes today. Household and industrial sectors presently burn fossil fuels to meet virtually all human needs around the world, including heating and cooling, transportation, utilities and appliances, power generation, and manufacturing. Carbon dioxide (CO_2) that rises in the air blankets the earth and traps heat. Global warming (due to long-term buildup of CO_2 in the atmosphere) changes weather that, in turn, affects the water base, food production, and world ecology over time.[1]

Global warming is a serious issue and problem today. Specifically, it slows down the process of continental glaciation and shrinks the polar icecaps. This can happen yearly or continuously, followed by higher sea levels that increase the likelihood of tsunamis (series of waves caused by displacement of a large volume of water) and El Ninos (oscillations of waves due to hot air over warm ocean waters in the eastern tropical Pacific).[2] It results in extreme drought and storms followed by floods that affect the water base and annual crops and eventually the global level of poverty in the world. It also causes ecological changes such as desertification, deforestation, faunal and floral anomalies, and wildlife relocations.[3]

In the absence of an immediate, tangible cost or benefit from them, many countries neglect environmental problems. Even worse, many countries ignore or fail to realize environmental impacts in the future because of inter-country conflicts of interest in economic growth among countries and intra-country conflicts of interests among domestic industries. Fast-growing Asian countries and economically mature countries in Europe cannot have the same interest in environmental control. In the intra-country case, the unionized coal miners and electrical workers in the United States, for example, protest constantly against the plan to regulate carbon emission by the U.S. Environmental Protection Agency (EPA). In the face of likely future problems due to global warming and ecological change expected, many countries and organizations such as the United Nations, IMF and World Bank have tried to prevent planetary disasters through international conferences and agreements. However, the agreements lack economic rationale.

This chapter examines a broad range of national and international agendas on environment and two related issues: global warming and water resources (GHE). Environmental disputes among countries reflect global economic disparities (GEDs) that prevail in this particular area. Reconciliation of inter-country conflicts of economic interest in connection with environmental controls requires international agreements that are based on economic rationale.

At present, oil prices keep plummeting. Cheaper oil will exacerbate global warming.

9.1 THE ENVIRONMENT AND GLOBAL WARMING

Global warming caused by greenhouse gases (carbon dioxide and methane) is the primary environmental problem. Most countries now take this problem seriously, partly as a result of serious efforts by the United Nations and other international organizations and on the basis of convincing evidence provided by scientists.

Among the objectives in the U.N. Environment Program, there are four notable areas for significant progress:

- eliminating ozone-depleting substances,
- phasing out lead in gasoline,
- increasing access to water supplies, and
- encouraging research into marine pollutants.

The EU is in favor of environmental regulations. Most of the western European countries heavily depend on natural gas supplied from Russia. Among EU member countries, Germany is on the top of the list. Germany has a good pipeline system for supply of natural gas from Russia under a long-term arrangement. In the absence of natural gas from Russia, CO_2 emissions of Germany could be much higher. The emissions of eastern European countries are high because of their coal consumption. Unlike

European countries, however, China, India, Japan, Russia, and the United States are the countries of large emissions of CO_2 from consumption of fossil fuel. Figure 9.1 exhibits their patterns of emissions. Carbon dioxide emissions by the United States have been always high. The amount of emissions by China was low but began to rise in 2000 and has exceeded the amount by the United States. At present, China and the United States are two major polluting countries. Japan is a country emitting a relatively large amount of carbon dioxide. India and Russia are also in the category of CO_2 emitters. Long-term CO_2 emissions in Japan remain to be seen because Japan plans to permanently shut down its existing nuclear power plants. India is expected to be a huge energy-consuming nation as a rapidly emerging economy. Among industrialized countries, in general, countries that strive for rapid economic growth are in the upper ranks of polluters.

At present, the global economy is in a long, drawn-out stagnation. The leading economies of the United States, Japan, and most EU countries do not show much positive sign of recovery. As the largest oil consuming nation in the world, the United States would pay a significant amount of cost for environmental controls. In comparison to Europe, the United States is not enthusiastic for environmental control. Overall, the world community realizes potential consequences of environmental problems. It does not seem to be a right time for the world community to discuss environmental issues.

As required to address interrelated subjects in this chapter, such as environment, global warming, and water resources, only a limited amount of research done by scientists is summarized here. Discussing such natural science subjects in detail is not the purpose of this book.

Many scientists are concerned about the global warming. Among substantial research done by scientists in this area, James Hansen at NASA's Goddard Institute for Space Studies (GISS) warned in 1988 that the average temperature of the earth's surface has increased by about 1.2–1.4 degrees Fahrenheit since 1900.[4] The Inter-governmental Panel on Climate Changes reports that the average temperature of the earth is expected to rise. After twenty-five years, Hansen asserted that the tipping point of global warming was near. On his graph, he showed an upward trend for the global temperature land-ocean index and a downward trend for sea ice conditions. This graph suggests that the world could be approaching a critical, planetary-scale transition to a different environment. Without reducing greenhouse gases significantly to achieve an optimum amount (350 ppm), he predicted that global ecology will be seriously damaged and sea levels drastically will rise.[5] In their article published in a recent issue of *Science*, Joughlin et al. (2014) suggest the onset of rapid collapse of glaciers in western Antarctica. Many ecologists assert that climate change now require the global community to take immediate actions. In

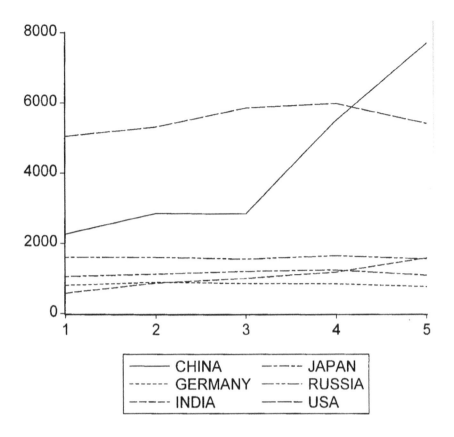

Figure 9.1.   Carbon Dioxide Emissions (1990 (1) - 2009 (5); in million metric tons). Note: 1 = 1990, 2 = 1995, 3 = 2000, 4 =2005, and 5 = 2009. Data: U.S. Census Bureau, Statistical Abstract of the United States: 2012, Washington, D.C.: U.S. GPO, p. 867.

the case of the United States, in a ten-year trend, temperature has increased steadily and the average annual temperature in 2006 was 55.0 degrees Fahrenheit, the highest level in 112 years. Nonetheless, the (Bush) administration rejected proposals to cap carbon dioxide emissions or impose carbon taxes.

While there are scientists, environmentalists, and ecologists who believe the earth is in dire straits, there are others who argue that the degree of global warming is exaggerated. Anti-environmentalists in the United States, especially interest groups on behalf of the coal industry, criticize the EPA for heavyhanded regulations that kill jobs and drive up energy costs. At present, the official position of the United States is based on an inconclusive scientific community but is leaning overall toward global warming as a serious threat. The National Climate Assessment of the

White House warned of the vulnerability from increasing risks from climate change and called for adaptation to it.[6]

9.2 INTERNATIONAL AGREEMENTS FOR ENVIRONMENTAL PROTECTION

The history of global environmental protection is long. There have been many conferences and agreements reached for this issue since the 1960s. Table 9.1 summarizes each of the main agreements. Note that the first four are concerned with radioactive contamination, wildlife, and hazardous materials.

This section focuses only on the primary international agreements about global warming from carbon dioxide and methane. The most important conference was held at Kyoto, Japan, in 1997, followed by a conference held at Copenhagen in 2009.[7] Prior to the general conference for the Kyoto accord, there were intense backstage negotiations initiated by a small group. The principle for the Kyoto Protocol was agreed on at the general conference in 1997. However, the agreement was vulnerable because it was based on inconclusive or controversial science. After ratification, countries were divided at implementation stage. The main reason for controversies was different economic interests among countries. Developing countries argued that countries face different economic situations, and the agreement was likely to be harmful to their economic growth and comparative advantage in international trade. Even in the United Sates, the Bush administration rejected the Kyoto proposals required to cap carbon dioxide emissions or impose carbon taxes.

In December 2009, a general conference of delegates from 193 countries met in Copenhagen but was unable to reach a conclusion. A smaller group of twenty-eight countries, the U.N. secretary general, and chairman of the EU agreed to draft a preliminary accord. China, India, Brazil, and South Africa held a separate meeting joined unexpectedly by the United States. China was uncomfortable with a provision on *transparency* that would allegedly result in an infringement of its sovereignty. The United States contended that the provision should be uniformly applicable to all countries and thus China's sovereignty would not be infringed upon. In response to the opposition to the accord drawn at the Copenhagen climate conference by the rest of the countries, it was agreed to *take note* of the accord rather than adopting any formal agreement. The twelve-paragraph document of final agreement was a statement of intention, not a binding agreement. The United States urged emerging countries, especially China and India, to eliminate carbon emissions, but these two countries argued that industrialized countries emit about 70 percent

Table 9.1. History of International Agreements for Environmental Protection

1.	Limited Test Ban Treaty (1963): Bans testing nuclear weapons in earth's atmosphere; has limited the amount of radioactive contamination in the environment.
2.	Convention on the International Trade in Endangered Species (CITES, 1975): Protection of wildlife by prohibiting trade of endangered species.
3.	Montreal Protocol (1987, amended in 1990 and 1992): Production and consumption of ozone-depleting compounds to be phased out by 2005.
4.	Basel Convention (1989): To prohibit the transfer of hazardous wastes from developed countries to underdeveloped countries.
5.	United Nations Framework Convention on Climate Change in Rio de Janeiro (1992): The first of 15 conferences to tackle global warming since 1992, it enabled environmental concerns to take center stage in global policy making.
6.	Kyoto Protocol (1997): Production of greenhouse gas to be phased out; rejected by the United States and Australia but ratified by Russia in 2004, 127 countries put the protocol into effect in 2005.
7.	Copenhagen Accord (2009): UN-sponsored climate summit.
8.	The Rio+20 in 2012 (C40 Climate Leadership Group Conference held along with the UN-sponsored Sustainable Development G-20 Summit in Rio de Janeiro): A conference of mayors representing 40 major cities in the world decided to reduce carbon dioxide emissions by one billion tons by 2030.
9.	Extension of the Kyoto Protocol (2012): The U.S. conference on climate changes held in Doha on December 7, 2012, decided to extend the Kyoto Protocol that was due to expire in 2012 for 8 years, until 2020.

of the total. A conference held in Mexico in January 2010 was also fruitless.

The Kyoto Protocol was scheduled to expire in 2012. There was an attempt to extend the deadline. The EU and thirty-eight other countries pledged to reduce greenhouse gas by 20 percent with respect to levels in 1990. However, the United States, Canada, Japan, Russia, New Zealand, and China rejected the extension. The United States opposed the extension because the protocol was not agreed to by China and other emerging countries as a binding commitment. This series of international failures is clearly a warning that the prospect of global progress to contain climate changes may now be permanently diminished.

Apart from the Kyoto and Copenhagen conferences, twenty-seven EU member countries held a conference in Bali, Indonesia, in January 2007. They agreed to reduce greenhouse gas emissions by at least 20 percent from 1990 levels by 2020 and to increase the use of renewable energy such as wind, solar, and hydropower for power needs and biofuels for road vehicles starting in March 2007. The legally binding thirteen-year target is to be achieved by burden sharing among the member countries, differentiated by country.

In brief, the EU has more easily achieved agreements on the environment because it depends on natural gas supplied by Russia. However, its efforts at global-scale environmental control have not been successful in reconciling differences in national interests. The overall position of the United States has been supportive but not as enthusiastic as the EU's. In the absence of significant alternative energy sources and as the biggest of energy consumer, it is costly for the United States to make a commitment on environmental problems in the form of a binding agreement. There is even a coal rush in the United States at present.[8] To developing countries, such as China, India, and Brazil, an international agreement for environmental protection contradicts their ultimate goal of economic growth.[9]

Given all these efforts through conferences, negotiations, and agreements for several decades, the overall result is disappointing. There are clearly different interests in the trade-off between environmental control and economic growth among countries. Some countries are in favor of environmental control, whereas others are against it or reluctant to participate actively at the expense of their economic growth. It is unreasonable to expect a reconciliation of conflicts of interests in the absence of any strong economic rationale in the foreseeable future.[10]

The fundamental problem of international conferences and agreements is not substantiated by pragmatic or applicable basics for enforcement and dispute settlement, such as the theory of *optimal* air pollution that might otherwise convince countries to cooperate.

9.3 GEOECONOMIC PERSPECTIVES ON GLOBAL WARMING

Carbon dioxide pollutes air, and polluted air leads to global warming. Clean air is a "public good," and thus polluted air can be characterized as a "public bad." The latter is not a concept frequently used in economics. However, this concept is useful for symmetrical arguments maintained in this section. If a public good is subject to a free-rider problem, then a public bad is subject to a "free-escapee" problem. A public good (or bad) is likely to involve economic externality, implying that behavior in pursuit of a free-ride or free-escape results in an adverse impact on the welfare of the community. Professor Ronald Coase, the Nobel Laureate in Economics in 1991, suggested efficiency of economic allocation in the presence of externality through competitive bargaining, if transaction cost is sufficiently low. This proposition is referred to as the "Coase theorem," which has often been illustrated by a competitive settlement of disputes in connection with pollution of water between an upstream user and downstream users by compensation from the former to the latter.[11] The same rationale may be applicable to posit a settlement of international disputes in the area of air polluted by a country for its economic growth. Air-polluting countries compensate for their shares of damaged air quality proportionately to the rest of the world in the form of, for example, monetary contributions to the international fund for environmental protection. However, the opportunity cost for environmental control is too big for a country in favor of economic growth, determined as the national first priority as in China and other countries in the face of high unemployment as in the United States at present. Furthermore, economic growth/unemployment could be structural in a country or cyclical in another.

This section discusses economic perspectives on pollution and global warming. It suggests that a *binding* agreement along with a strong enforcement mechanism for reconciliation of inter-country disputes is possible only with mutuality on the economic rationale acceptable to both sides of countries. Without this, any attempt to resolve environmental issues on an international scale will be futile.

9.3.1. Nature of Global Warming

It is difficult to apply a concept such as *global* warming uniformly applicable to all countries. The reasons are as follows:

(1) Conflicts of Interest between Industrialized and Industrializing Countries

The primary energy source in the EU is natural gas, a clean form of energy. The EU can easily be in favor of environmental control, whereas

China and India want their economies to grow fast in order to feed 1.3 and 1.2 billion people, respectively. Even for a highly developed country like the United States, it is difficult to change the conventional pattern of household consumption and industrial structure to reduce burning oil and coal.

According to Newton's law of gravity in physics, the force of gravity that attracts two masses to each other is proportional to the product of their masses and inversely to (the square of) their distance apart. A given *mass* (for example, EU's desire for environmental control) may be heavy (strong), but another mass (China's desire for environmental control) may be light (weak). The *distance* (difference) between two different countries with very different (opposite) interests is far apart. A small value for the numerator and a large value for the denominator, in accordance with Newton's formula, yield a small value for *gravity* (i.e., poor or no cooperation between the countries). Given this rationale for conflicts unresolved between the two countries, it is logically difficult to expect an international agreement on the environmental problems. From this respect, the Copenhagen failure was expected. If, however, the density of smog and yellow sand dust from the desert are intense in Beijing, for example, the desire for environmental control may become strong in China, and attitudes toward conflicts of interest may change. In fact, the United States and China, the two leading air-polluting countries in the world, agreed to tighten pollution standards to curb greenhouse gas emissions later in 2013.[12]

(2) Lack of Perception about Tangible Benefits from Environmental Control

There are mutual gains from free trade for trading countries, in accordance with all trade theories: Ricardian law of comparative advantage (classical theory), neoclassical theory (reciprocal demand curve analysis) and modern theory (the Heckscher-Ohlin-Samuelson theory). In this case, the gains are tangible and have become incentives for trade promotions through multilateral free trade agreements since the GATT of 1947. In the event of trade disputes, there is now an enforcement mechanism and dispute settlement procedures under the Uruguay Round of 1994. Unlike in the past, the panel's decision is *binding*. This quasi-judicial process is based on guidelines dictated by the twenty-seven provisions directly relevant to dispute settlement, including a stringent time limit on each stage of the process, transparency, compensation, and retaliation.[13] The WTO system works remarkably.

However, benefits from environmental control are intangible. There is no strong incentive or clear scientific basis for an enforcement mechanism to motivate countries toward environmental protection. In the absence of incentives and enforcement for environmental protection, it is difficult to expect countries to observe international agreements. There must be an improvement in the scientific measurement of environmental benefit and loss to convince the majority of world citizens who believe that global warming is all up to the sun.

(3) Externality and Moral Hazard

Perfect competition ensures a Pareto optimum, a situation where no other strategy will make a country better off without making other countries worse off.[14] However, such an optimum is not valid in conditions of externality, a phenomenon of a divergence between private and social costs (or between private gains and social gains). As a public bad, global warming involves a free-escapee problem and moral hazard such as ignorance of an agreement or negligence of responsibility. Countries need to figure out the way to minimize moral hazard.

9.3.2. Disputes and Reconciliations

An international relationship *per se* is complex by nature. Different countries occupy different circumstances. Global warming is only one of many issues in a country. In addition, domestic politics in every country are transitory. An international agreement supported by the previous regime may be overlooked by the incoming regime. One cannot expect all countries to faithfully observe an international agreement all the time. It is also questionable whether the world as a whole should uniformly pursue clean air at the expense of economic growth and development, especially given high levels of income inequality between and within countries and many cases of absolute poverty.

Global warming is not a conventional economic problem. As the cause of the global warming problem reflects global economic disparities (GEDs) among countries, however, any attempt and approach to reconcile such differences is valuable for the world community. In economics, a Cournot solution (the intersection point between reaction functions) and the game theory (e.g., a clean air, clean air strategy pair locked in a prisoner's dilemma) between two distinct groups of countries are regarded as powerful approach to the reconciliation. Given the different economic interests of different countries, and in the absence of a detailed, binding agreement and strong enforcement mechanism, however, the appropriate strategy pair of game theory will not readily emerge without incentives.

As discussed earlier, the Coase theorem is concerned with the property rights to buy and sell in the market. The theorem suggests a settlement of disputes between disputants that will lead an efficient allocation of resources through competitive bargaining. The competitive bargaining that is promoted by an incentive is applicable to externality and moral hazard that are the barriers to perfect competition. The rational here can be applied to global warming. Every country may be allowed to discharge CO_2 gas subject to a fine that induces countries to minimize air pollution around the world.

Recently, the World Bank suggested an idea similar to the proposition addressed in this chapter and a few additional suggestions, such as investment for clean air in cities, pro-environmental agreement, and elimination of the subsidy paid for burning fossil fuel in urban areas. It may also minimize problems of externality and moral hazard. For example, every country would be allowed to discharge CO_2 gas subject to a fine. The resulting fund could be used for scientific research on environmental protection or for a multinational campaign to alleviate poverty in poor countries. Any attempt to reconcile conflicts of interest among countries only through enforcement of regulations in international agreements may be ineffective, especially when global economic disparities strongly prevail. The Kyoto agreement has drifted along without tangible results for almost two decades.

9.3.3. The Optimal Pollution

It is impossible to achieve the goal of a pollution-free world. As indicated earlier in this section, there are two opposing interests connected to global warming: environmental protection and economic growth. Global warming will eventually be devastating to our living conditions on earth, whereas global economic growth will slow down and poverty will probably ensue. It is imperative to find the optimal level of pollution that reconciles the trade-off problem of environmental protection.

The optimum level of pollution should logically fall somewhere between these two contradictory choices. One is a positive function of the sub-cost from sluggish economic growth (on the vertical axis) with respect to degree of policy enforcement (on the horizontal axis). As policy measures intensify, the sub-cost increases. The other is a negatively sloped sub-function of global cost with respect to the intensity of environmental policy enforcement. An aggressive enforcement (e.g., progressive penalties levied for failing to meet a target pollution level) reduces the sub-cost from CO_2. Given the two opposed interests taken by two different groups of countries, the global cost function of environmental problems is the sum of these two different sub-cost functions. The optimal degree of environmental control corresponds to the minimum point of the total global cost function (the sum of the two sub-cost functions) of global warming.[15]

9.4 WATER RESOURCES

In the early life of earth, there was a period when land masses began to split into large continental groups and continued to split over time to form today's configuration.[16] This period of continental drift was followed by ice ages when, for example, the region of the Sahara Desert was transformed from tropical rainforest to arid wasteland.[17] Earth has continually changed through surface processes, such as climate, volcanism, avalanches, landslides, forest fires, erosions, and so on.

Three-fourths of the earth is covered by water. However, people settled in areas where fresh water was available. History confirms that civilizations grew mostly near rivers. The Nile in Egypt, the Tigris and Euphrates in Mesopotamia, the Yangtze and Hwang Ha in China, and the Ganges and Indus in India are rivers where the largest ancient cultures of the world flourished. One cannot think of European culture independently of the Rhine and Danube. The Amazon in South America is the lifeline of that continent, and countless smaller rivers around the world are equally critical for human life. Many major cities today were once small towns located near rivers or lakes. From an airplane or a river cruise, tourists can easily see villages in lush green lands on both banks of the Nile flowing through a vast gray *desert* land.[18 ,19] Industrial countries in mild or continental climates (with water) and African and Mideast countries in tropical or desert climates (without water) are the façade of earth today.

History also suggests that ancient communities had no environmental problem like global warming today that seriously affects water resources.

This section focuses on water shortage. Needless to say, water is absolutely essential for humans. Without it, a human body cannot biologically exist. Water is critical in economic activities for both household and industrial purposes. In general, there are two different types of countries—industrial and agricultural, and two different types of industries within a country—rural (agricultural) and urban. For both, since they consume considerable amounts of water, the hydrological cycle from surface storage and oceans and evaporation to precipitation is prerequisite. However, the cycle is beyond the control of man. Given the expected future shortage of water in many countries, there are problems of inter-country and inter-industry water allocations. (1) The former may become a politically and economically serious problem in the future. Imagine the situation of over 2.5 billion people in both China and India soon, who need water and food. Competition to secure water is tacitly going on among countries. Information on water resources is treated as strategically sensitive in many countries. The global water base in the long run has diminished. Information on water resources is a military secret in India and is not publicly accessible in China. (2) On the latter, a country could choose either more water for agricultural products or more for urban facilities.

Southern California, for example, faces such a choice problem. Cost of living there has sharply increased in recent decades. The choice appears to be more water for the agricultural sector.

In terms of economics, a shortage of water is an excess demand for water. Detailed information on this subject, however, is not directly relevant to this book and is partly beyond the scope of economics. It may be a misjudgment to expect that environmental problems, global warming, and water shortage will be resolved anytime in the near future. Conflicts of economic interest among countries and within a country are more complex than imagined.

NOTES

1. U.S. National Oceanic and Atmospheric Administration confirms that the burning of fossil fuels is primarily responsible for an increase in greenhouse gases (carbon dioxide and methane). According to the National Climatic Data Center, the warmest year in the United States for the past 112 years was 2006. The average temperatures projected over the period of 1950–2050, under the assumption of CO2 emissions maintained at the current level, exhibit an upward trend as close as 45 degrees. See Oxford University Press (2011), p. 15. In its *Surface Temperature Analysis*, the NASA reports a similar pattern. For global warming and water resources, see the analysis on climate changes in IMF's *World Economic Outlook*, October 2007 and subsequent issues.

2. Sea levels have actually risen worldwide by about 8 inches since 1900. See Oxford University Press (2011), p. 15. On May 28, 2008, the five coastal countries bordering on the Arctic Ocean—Canada, Denmark, Norway, the Russian Federation and the United States—met in Greenland to discuss the potential impact of climate change and the melting of ice that stands at the threshold level on the vulnerable ecosystem.

3. In contrast to the fifth great extermination, ecologists Anthony Barnosky et al. (*Nature*, 2012) predicted that the sixth great extermination of creatures, especially mammals of about 80 out of 5,570, is on the way within 300 years. Excessive hunting, reckless fishing, expansion of germs and viruses, foreign species, and climate changes due to greenhouse gas are the causes of the extermination.

4. *Washington Post*, January 10, 2007 (W), A1 and A4.

5. James Hansen warned about global warming at the U.S. Senate hearing on June 23, 1988. He delivered a speech at the Press Club titled "Global Warming 20 Years Later: Tipping Points Near."

6. See Joughlin, Smith, and Medley (2014) and National Climate Assessment (2014).

7. For a brief history on arrangements for environmental protection prior to the Kyoto Protocol (1997), including U.N. framework conventions on climate change, see table 9.1.

8. Nonetheless, the United States has strictly implemented policies for environmental control under self-auspices and has schedules for continued regulations. About forty coal power plants are scheduled to shut down in the near future and technologies for fuel efficiency and hybrid vehicles have made a significant contribution to clean air.

9. There are some developing countries that are attempting to shift from coal to wind for power generation. China, for example, has a plan for generation of 100K MW of electricity by wind power.

10. It has been known that political institutions determine policies concerning environmental regulation in the absence of economic rationale.

11. The upstream users compensate for the amount of water pollution to the downstream users for the settlement. This proposition is referred to as the "Coase theorem." See Coase (1960).

12. See endnote 10.

13. *Washington Post,* July 11, 2013, p. A13.

14. See Chung (2006), pp. 154–59.

15. The Pareto optimality is equivalent to the Nash equilibrium in game theory, that is, the optimal strategy pair in the situation of mixture of conflicting versus parallel interests in social interactions.

16. Assuming that the total cost function is quadratic, the minimum total cost requires the necessary and sufficient conditions for the minimization of the function by elementary calculus. See Chung (2006), pp. 194–200. The concept of global environmental cost is based on social cost in connection with optimal choice. See Becker (1968), Becker and Mulligan (2003), and many others for earlier work on the social cost.

17. Oxford University Press (2011), p. 4.

18. Barraclough (1998), pp. 4–5.

19. Water was critical for Egypt to the extent that the Egyptian government relocated even ancient temples thousands of years old, Abu Simbel and Philae, in order to create Lake Nasser in the Aswan area.

TEN

Food, Population, and Poverty

Food is essential for human living, and poverty is ubiquitous across human societies, though undesirable. Severe shortages of food over time in a country are a direct cause of poverty. Both food and poverty are correlated with the population, a primary concern of demographers. Some demographers suggest the possibility of an economic cataclysm in connection the trend of population and social welfare programs in the future. From the global standpoint, economic disparity (GED) prevails in each area—food, population, and poverty.

The theory of consumer behavior is a major branch of microeconomics. There are two fundamental laws of consumer behavior in the theory of household consumption. One is the law of demand, and the other is Engel's law. The former states a negative relationship between the price of a particular good and the quantity of the good demanded (price effect). It is generally known that demand for an agricultural product (food) is relatively inelastic with respect to price. Inelastic demand for food implies that demand for an agricultural good makes slow adjustments with respect to price variations in the market, and thus any government pricing policy is relatively ineffective. It is also known that as the price of farm goods increases, only the expenditure for food by poor countries increases, and the number of people who starve increases.

There is another law, the so-called Engel's law. In a study done in 1857, C. L. Ernst Engel (1821–1896) established a law suggesting that the proportion of the budget spent on food decreased as household income increased, implying that a poor family spends relatively more income for food than a rich family. This law, often referred to as Engle's law, suggests that the budgetary share of food consumption by the poor is relatively larger.[1]

Professor Hendrick Houthakker (1957), who examined forty budget studies in thirty countries on the one hundredth anniversary of Engel's work, confirmed the validity of Engel's law. The U.S. Bureau of Labor Statistics (1964) has confirmed that Engel's law holds for U.S. household consumption expenditures, as shown in detailed studies of not only food but also clothing, shelter, fuel, light, appliances, education, medical care, and automobiles. This law is still widely accepted today. Economists continue to investigate Engel's law across other countries in the world. Differences in the pattern of household expenditure between rich and poor countries contain serious geoeconomic implications for global economic disparity (GED). Studies on consumer demand at the international level also continue today.[2]

There are domestic and international markets for food. Both demand for food and supply of food are subject to market conditions. However, the latter is significantly affected by nature. Such a uniqueness of the supply side is only partially a domain of economics but requires drawing multidisciplinary attention.

This chapter investigates three related topics that reflect a multiplicity of issues relating to food, poverty and economic cataclysm attributed to the declining trends of population in many countries.

10.1 FOOD

Most countries have an independent governmental department that works exclusively for improvement of farm income and expansion of home and foreign markets for agricultural products. In the United States, for example, the Department of Agriculture has many divisions, encompassing poverty and hunger, production, conservation of soil, water, forests and natural resources, and exports of agricultural goods. The Foreign Agricultural Service (FAS) is responsible for overseas market information, export assistance, and food assistance programs through its offices posted more than sixty embassies.[3]

There are unique features associated with the agricultural industry in a country:

1. Natural forces such as storms, droughts and extreme heat and cold can result in detrimental effects on world granaries. There is also the manmade global warming caused by air pollution that results in higher sea levels, coastal flooding from melting glaciers, and shortages of farm products.[4] As discussed in the previous chapter, many countries are unwilling to participate in international efforts to prevent global warming at the expense of their economic growth.

2. From the economics standpoint, consumers' demand for food is inelastic, and the inflationary effects of food shortages are strong, especially for people in poor countries.

3. Many countries protect their agricultural industry by means of various policies, including subsidies. Subsidies provided by large agricultural countries distort international food markets. Payment of subsidies to promote exports by a country is prohibited by the GATT of 1947 and now by the WTO agreement. Disputes between the United States and Europe about subsidy payments are well-known.[5] In the case of the United States, there is a provision for a countervailing duty (Section 701), as specified in the Trade Remedy Laws in the Omnibus Trade and Competitiveness Act of 1988.[6]

4. Despite relief efforts conducted by rich countries, international agencies such as the United Nations, and philanthropic and religious groups, poverty still prevails all over the world. Food is an absolute necessity but is not always distributed to needy people who cannot afford to pay for it in poor countries. Corrupt regimes in poor nations often divert food provided by rich countries for their own political and military purposes.

According to the Food and Agriculture Organization of the United Nations (FAO), agriculture uses approximately 38 percent of the land surface in the world, divided into arable land, permanent cropland, and pasture. The FAO suggests that per capita production has increased mainly due to better irrigation and more applications of fertilizer in the past fifty years. However, the world still needs to produce more food as population grows and consumption patterns change but more land is used for energy production.[7] The specter of Malthusian limits (see section 10.3) is still a potent threat. The validity of economic principles generally presupposes the existence of competitive markets. Unilateral transfers, foreign aid, and grants reduce starvation only in the short run. A global shortage of food would cause political crises in many countries, especially in the third world. It is necessary for donating countries and organizations to establish long-term policies or programs to induce recipient countries to gradually move toward competitive markets.

10.1.1 World Grain Production

Food includes many items: grain, meat, dairy products, fish, vegetables and fruit. This section focuses on grain. Table 10.1 shows production, exports, and imports of grains broken down into wheat, rice, corn, and coarse grain by country. In general, countries with more arable land acreage produce and export more grains, whereas countries with less acreage and a high population density consume more and import more. Rice is produced and consumed mostly by countries in the Eastern hemisphere, whereas wheat is produced and consumed largely in the Western hemisphere. The top half of the table shows crops produced by selected major

agricultural countries. They are mostly crop exporting countries. There are no data available for corn production or for exports and imports of coarse grains. The bottom half of the table shows imports (excess demand or shortages) of wheat, rice, and corn by poor countries. The numbers appear to be small, but actual amounts should be large in light of their economic size.

10.1.2 Prices of Grains

In economics, the agricultural industry in a country is characterized as competitive on the grounds that each of the agricultural goods is homogeneous, and there are many producers and many consumers in the country. A competitive market determines the equilibrium price. An international grain market is a collective market of competitive domestic food markets and determines the global equilibrium price. Countries should trade food at this equilibrium price. However, subsidies paid by the government for export promotion result in a higher price to domestic consumers and a lower price to foreign consumers.

Like other commodities, the price of food in the world market is subject to changes over time. There are two different causes of the price dynamics: cost-push and demand-pull. The price of food increases because the supply schedule (the marginal cost curve) shifts to the left. The former shifts the supply schedule to the left and/or the demand schedule shifts upward.[8] Unlike many other goods, however, demand for food is relatively inelastic. Given the uniqueness in inelastic demand for food (a constant by assumption for simplicity), the prices of farm goods are predominantly determined by factors associated with the supply schedule, such as energy, storage, and transportation costs and external factors like climate in a particular year. However, there are many cases where the demand for food is by no means separable from the supply side of food in the process of price determination.

Specifically,

1. Higher costs of oil, fertilizers, transportation, and storage of agricultural products increase the price of food. Due to high prices of oil, the United States, which exports almost two-thirds of its corn, has increased production of corn to meet both the industrial demand for biofuels (ethanol) and the demand for animal feed.
2. Many countries protect their agricultural industry. As discussed above, subsidies paid by large agricultural countries distort the

Table 10.1. World Crop Production, Exports, and Imports (in millions of metric tons)

	Wheat			Rice			Corn		Coarse Grain		
	Q	X	M	Q	X	M	QX	M	Q	X	M
U.S.	60.4	34.7		7.1			49.5		348.5		
Canada	26.8	17.0							22.5		
EU-27	138.6	22.0						6.5	155.3		
Russia	61.8	4.0							31.8		
Ukraine	20.9	3.5					5.5		24.1		
China	115.1			136.6					163.6		
India	80.7			89.1			2.5		33.9		
Brazil	5.0			7.7					58.4		
Argentina	11.0	8.5		0.7			14.5		28.0		
Australia	21.9	14.5		0.1					11.1		
Turkey	18.5	3.0		0.4					11.2		
Egypt			10.0					5.4			
Morocco			3.9								
Nigeria			3.7			1.9		2.4			
Algeria											
Vietnam					6.0						
Cambodia					0.1						
Bangladesh						1.4					
Philippines						1.2					
Cote d'Ivoire						0.9					
Paraguay							1.7				
World	648.2			440.1					1,109.6		

Notes: World Crop Production (Q): 2009–2010, in millions of metric tons
    Exports (X): 2010
    Imports (M): 2010.
    Source: U.S. Census Bureau, *Statistical Abstract of the United States*:
2012, p. 860.
    U.S. Department of Agriculture, *Economic Research Service*.

international price structure. Higher domestic prices due to subsidies often fail to increase agricultural production. Exports of agricultural products have been restricted by some major food-producing countries in order to stabilize their domestic food prices by means of export quotas and tariffs. Items affected by such restrictions are: (a) wheat (by Argentina, fourth largest wheat export country in the world; Russia, sixth largest wheat export country; Ukraine; Kazakhstan and China, eighth largest wheat export country), (b) soybeans (by Argentina), (c) rice (by China, sixth largest rice export country in the world; Thailand; India; Vietnam, third largest rice export country); United States; Pakistan; Cambodia; Indonesia and Egypt), and (d) corn (by the United States, the largest export country). Exports of corn produced for industrial purpose is often controversial in importing counties. The impact of their supply shocks on prices of agricultural products in global markets is enormous.

3. Inclement weather reduced world production of agricultural products for the past several years, followed by a higher price of food. In the recent past, there was a long drought in Australia (fifth largest wheat export country). The drought reduced cereal stocks to their lowest level in twenty-five years. Water shortages and rapid urbanization in China have resulted in the substitution of beans imported from South American countries, especially from Brazil, for beans produced in China. This substitution has expedited deforestation in the Amazon.

4. There have been significant dietary changes in some emerging countries as their incomes increase. Many consumers, especially in China and India, the two most populous countries in the world, have switched from starchy foods to more meat and dairy products. As the economy grows rapidly, per capita meat consumption in China has increased 40 percent since 1980. Changes in dietary pattern have increased an excess supply of starchy food and demand for grain as fodder as the price of starchy food decreases.

5. Information and transportation technologies accelerate speculative transactions of agricultural goods in international grain markets. If the dollar becomes weaker, their prices are expected to soon be higher. Countries are then motivated to import food as soon as

possible. The world price of grains began to increase after the second half of 2006. Japan (fourth largest wheat importing country), the Philippines (second largest rice importing country), and Taiwan attempted to secure grains earlier than in the past.

Each year, the FAO releases the food price index (FPI). It measures the aggregated price of food. Figure 10.1 shows the FPI that is the average of the five commodity group price indices weighted with average export shares of each group for 2002–2004. The five-commodity group includes meat, dairy, cereals, vegetable oil, and sugar. These measures reflect consumption patterns of food today. Among the five items, cereals that include wheat, maize (corn), and rice are the most basic items, consumed by all households, rich or poor. The composite index of cereal prices is based on two consecutive observations, one from July in the previous year to June in the current year for wheat, and the other from January to December in each year for rice. As shown in the figure, the FPI for all items *steadily* increased up to 2011 and decreased in 2012.

Sudden food shortages and higher food prices have intensified speculation about imminent crises in the global food market. Climate changes in the world will likely result in severe shortages of food production and eventually a major crisis. According to the FAO, the grain price index was 244.8, higher by 44 percent in comparison to the index in January 2010. International prices of corn and wheat were higher by 80 percent than those in the previous year. The World Bank also warned that prices of food and grain in international markets are dangerously high and that the high prices catalyze opposing political interests across the world. Overall, the FPI is high. A high price of food directly affects the poor, who spend most of their income for food (about 80 percent in underdeveloped countries). They are severely afflicted by hunger, long-term poverty, and malnutrition from consuming a smaller quantity and lower quality of food.

The world economy has been experiencing a potentially long-term stagnation amid a massive financial crisis initiated in the United States. In the event of a radical increase in food prices in the foreseeable future, the impact on the world economy will be disastrous. The ongoing crisis will likely be aggravated by global inflation, further retardation in economic growth, and an increase in food expenditure by poor countries accompanied by higher wages demanded by workers in food-producing countries.[9]

Price variations alter the terms of trade affecting international commerce in food. Trade plays an important role in stabilizing the global food market, which is subject to frequent disturbances of climate in agriculture-based countries. Fortunately, the prices of agricultural products now appear to be stabilized to some extent.

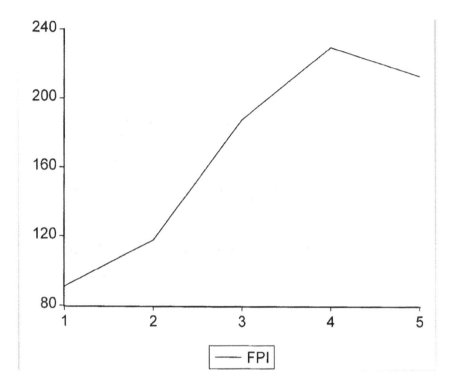

Figure 10.1.   UNFAO Food Price Index, (2000(1) - 2012 (4)). Note: 1 = 2000, 2 = 2005, 3 = 2010, 4 = 2011, 5 = 2012. Data: Food and Agriculture Organization of the United Nations, FAO Statistical Yearbook, FAO Food Price Index, 2012.

During the global crisis prevailing at present, it is difficult to project the trend of any economic variable. However, there are a few important trends to consider for speculation on the global food crisis in the future:

    a. Production of crops in the world has recently increased, but their stocks are low.

    b. Arable land has shrunk as a result of urbanization in many countries.

    c. Industrial demand for agricultural goods continues to increase.

10.2 POVERTY

Poverty, and often famine, has remained a serious problem throughout the world since ancient times.[10] According to the UNDP (United Nations Development Programme), 1.2 billion people live on 1.25 dollars or less a day. In terms of its poverty index that takes into account deprivation in health and education, almost 1.5 billion people in 91 developing countries are living in poverty.[11] They live in despair and frustration with hardly any hope for the future.

As the economic situation of lack of money or material possessions, poverty does not follow the same criteria applicable uniformly to all countries. In other words, the standards of poverty or low-income brackets in the United States and Europe are not the same as those of Africa, South America, and Asia. In the United States, for example, a family of four with an annual income of 20,000 dollars (21,756 in the official statistics) is at the poverty level. A family of four with that annual income is not considered poor in underdeveloped continents. Such quantitative and qualitative differences in poverty between advanced and underdeveloped countries complicate poverty issues at the global level. There is no statistical criterion for measuring the degree of poverty that is uniformly applicable to all countries. Even without the criterion, it is clear that the GED prevails in the poverty area.

Economists employ the Lorenz curve to measure the inequality of wealth distribution. This technique may be used to estimate the degree of global economic inequality. If a few people own most of the wealth in an imaginary country, the majority of people in that country are likely to be poor. Given the purpose of this book, an attempt to measure degree of poverty in terms of the Lorenz curve is unnecessarily specific. Even without any statistical work, the Lorenz curves for most of African countries are supposed to be close enough to the horizontal axis and the vertical axis. It is sufficient here to discuss the global status of poverty in terms of per capita national income along with production and shortages of food by country.

Without using any sophisticated statistical inferences, Africa (except South Africa), southern Asia (except Malaysia, Singapore, and Thailand), and Central and South America (except Mexico, Argentina, Brazil, Chile, and Uruguay) are the poverty areas identified readily in terms of the per capita gross national income (GNI) available in publications by the World Bank and other international organizations. Compare 160 dollars for the per capita GNI in Congo with 65,430 dollars for GNI in Switzerland. Even without index numbers to measure poverty levels, these data are self-explanatory as to how people live in the world. Many countries do not publish the data, presumably because they are poorer than others or do not know how to estimate their GNI. Of course, per capita GNI does not necessarily reflect the quality of life. Although per capita income is small, many islands in the South Pacific are known as a paradise to both natives and tourists.

For most poor people in a country, food is on the top of the list for their needs. Education, health care, and social welfare are virtually luxuries for them. Affluent countries have helped poor countries through their foreign aid programs. International agencies, including the United Nations, and religious and philanthropic organizations, have been providing food and medical services as part of their humanitarian assistance for over half a century. However, poverty prevails without any structural improvement in recipient countries. Most of recipient countries have arable land and work forces. Therefore, it is necessary for donor countries and organizations to reorient recipient countries by switching the mode for expected generosity to self-sufficiency at least in food. In addition to existing programs of the World Bank, including infrastructure improvement in poor countries, a fund available to countries in poverty for their gradual market exposure may facilitate alleviating poverty.

10.3 POPULATION

In "An Essay on the Principle of Population," 1798, Thomas Malthus (1766–1834) proposed that food increases at an arithmetic progression whereas population increases at a geometric progression. Controversial among contemporary economists, the two-centuries-old proposition implies that a shortage of food will be perpetual unless checked by famine and disease. It was a key insight of pre–Industrial Revolution demography.

Population is the primary subject of demographers. There is an areal intersection between demography and economics regarding issues such as starvation, natural resources, and social welfare. In addition to shortages of food for feeding over seven billion people (6.9 and 7.6 billion as of 2010 and 2020, respectively, in the world), the problems of depleting water tables, eroding soil, melting glaciers, and vanishing fish stocks are typically attributed to the behavior of human populations. On the other hand, there is a serious problem in the area of social welfare in certain countries, especially as their population declines in the long run. This section examines economic catastrophe expected in the future.

10.3.1 Population in the World and the Malthusian Law

As discussed in the previous section, the Malthusian law suggests a positive correlation between population and food at two different rates, a geometric progression for the former and an arithmetic progression for the latter.[12] The law implies that, if population growth is unchecked, starvation is an inevitable consequence and people are motivated to work harder. Thus, countries are tempted to conquer the world for more shares of world markets. From the geoeconomic standpoint, much of the European history of geographical exploration, territorial expansion, and colonization is explained by a series of economic implications such as securing raw materials.

Table 10.2 presents world population by continent, actual and projected at intervals of ten years from 1980 to 2050. The population increases at almost a constant rate of growth throughout the period. There is no such pattern of geometric progression for the growth of population, as proposed by Malthus. In terms of share by continent, the population density ranges from the highest in Asia to the lowest in Europe. The density share of Asia is approximately 60 percent without any substantial changes over time, probably because of the large population in China and India. The low density of population existing in Europe is projected to decline significantly. According to the U.S. Bureau of the Census, populations in North America and South America remain almost the same. In the case of the United States, the population size passed 250 million in 1990, increased to 310 million in 2010, and is projected to 341 million in 2020 by the U.S. Bureau of the Census. The U.S. population is now the third largest after the populations of China and India. Note that immigrants are a large share in the case of the United States. Other countries where population is expected to grow in the future are mostly poor countries. This table shows that the population density in rich continents is relatively low, whereas density in poor continents is high and projected to become higher.

The percentage share of population in Africa with respect to the world total has steadily increased and is expected to grow in the future. It was less than 15 percent in 2000 but is expected to be about 20 percent by 2050. Without significant growth in the African economy, population growth implies that the poverty level in Africa will rise. In the absence of adequate social insurance, welfare, and pensions in most of African countries at present, the poverty level is beyond our imagination. Terms such as *direct premium*, health *expenditures*, *practicing physicians*, *benefit contribution funds*, and *benefits paid by pension funds*, and so on, are not appropriate.

Apart from table 10.2, demographers estimate that global population will reach nine billion before 2050.[13] Historians state that world population has not decreased since the Black Death of the fourteenth century. Improvement of medical care and sanitary facilities, especially in developing countries and with the help of international organizations, have spared many lives. Except for politically engineered mass starvations under the Stalin regime in the1930s in the USSR, Mao's Great Leap Forward in the late 1950s in China, and some starvation incidents in Africa more recently, population growth and massive starvation have been the general perception about population before the twentieth century. Paul Ehrlich (1968), a biologist and demographer, regarded as a modern Malthusian, asserted the likelihood of massive starvation in 1975 as a result of population explosion.[14] He also gave a dire warning about population growth and limited resources in the world. Recently, Kunzig (2011) suggests that world population is still growing by about 80 million each year and that, although it is slowing down, the population explosion is far

Table 10.2. World Population by Continent, 1950–2050 (population in millions: growth and shares in percent)

	World		Africa		Asia		Europe		North America		South America	
	N	g	N	g	N	g	N	g	N	g	N	g
1950	2,557											
1960	3,042											
1970	3,713											
1980	4,453	19.9	479	10.8	2,644	59.4	695	15.6	371	8.4	242	5.4
1990	5,289	18.8	630		3,189		723		424		297	
2000	6,089	15.1	803	13.2	3,691	60.6	730	12.0	486.	8.0	348	5.7
2010	6,853	12.6	1,015		4,133		734		539		440	
2020	7,597	10.9	1,261	16.6	4,531	59.6	731	9.6	595	7.8	477	6.3
2030	8,259	8.7	1,532		4,841		718		648		504	
2040	8,820	6.8	1,827		5,049		698		695		489	
2050	9,284	NA	2,138	19.7	5,167	58.9	671	7.2	739	8.1	520	5.5

Source: U.S. Bureau of the Census, *Statistical Abstract of the United States*, 2012, p. 835.

N = Number of population, g = Rate of growth.

from over with seven billion people in 2011 and probably nine billion in 2045.[15] Mathematical algorithms would facilitate our understanding of demographers' complex projections on population. What they suggest is an increase in population at decreasing rates over time, presumably because of a trade-off between child mortality and fertility. This relationship implies that couples who face increasingly serious *economic* hardship, combined with pessimism about their future living conditions, have fewer children as their mortality declines. In developed countries, (e.g., Europe) there may be a *quality* of life factor encouraging fewer children in higher income families, so that each child can receive more. A majority of demographers seems to agree that population will level off or even fall by the second half of this century. They suggest that a couple has to produce about 2.1 children to replace themselves, but replacement fertility among young people of today is insufficient. As Ehrlich wrote, the rate of population growth was at a peak but, except for the case of African countries, fertility rates around the world had begun to decline rapidly by the early 1970s. The replacement rate of the U.S. population was 2.03 but only counting immigrants.

Many countries are vulnerable. These include some European nations, Russia, Canada, East Asian countries (including Japan, South Korea and China), India, and many Latin American countries. In eastern and western Europe, Russia, Canada, and the United States, native-born citizens are not reproducing fast enough to replace themselves. Fertility rates in East Asia, including Japan, China, and the main cities in India are already below replacement level. The overall projection on replacement fertility is pessimistic, and demographic transitions that usually take a generation are not smooth enough for the long run. Demographers go on to ask vexing questions about the global capacity for natural resources in the future. However, this topic is largely beyond the particular economic focus of the present book.

Contrary to the Malthusian predictions, some writers argue that food stocks are sufficient to feed the entire world population due to a dramatic improvement of production in the twentieth century during the Green Revolution.[16] In the past, spread of corn and potatoes following the discovery of the New World helped banish starvation in Europe. What is lacking in reality is a system of efficient allocations of food. Food does not reach to the needy people in certain poor countries. In addition to domestic and international market failures due to protection of the agricultural industry in almost every country, food is often used as a political tool between countries. Many trade disputes have occurred among food export countries.[17] Issues in connection with affluent and poor classes within a country and in the world have always been serious in every country throughout human history. Large numbers of people starve to death each year even today. Given the uncertainty about the future, on natural disasters and global warming, however, Malthus' dismal theorem will remain as a postulated hypothesis. It is also reasonable to hypothesize the consequences of the opposite case of the Malthus prediction on population. Population size is an important direct determinant of poverty. There is a trade-off phenomenon. Too large a total population may lead to not enough food per capita. But too small a working population may lead to a tax base too small to support an adequate social welfare system.

10.3.2 Population and Economic Cataclysm

Country-specific data show irregular patterns of population. However, the worldwide decline of population (table 10.2) is the fact that fixes largely the pattern of population in the future. Birthrates have begun to fall in many countries (but not throughout the world). In mathematical terms, their population increases at rapidly decreasing rates at present and is expected to decrease at increasing rates in the near future. A question arises here: Will there then be enough people in the younger working generation to support the older retirees through social insurance and pensions or direct family contributions as in East Asian societies traditionally (but less so now)? Most research on population has focused on the Malthusian proposition. Today, however, there are some demographers who study social safety net issues due to a growing inter-generational population gap, especially in more developed countries.

According to the United Nations and U.S. Bureau of the Census, roughly one-quarter of the world population will be sixty-five years old and above by 2025 amid a rapidly declining population in the younger generation. Given low birth rates across the world, except in the United States, millions of poor elders will face a dark future without retirement benefits—social security, pensions, and health insurance. Table 10.3 exhibits insurance and pensions available only in developed countries. China is expected to experience the worst economic catastrophe in less than twenty years, probably because of its one-child rule (it is now changing this coercive policy) in effect since 1979.[18] As mentioned in the previous section, population has already begun to decline in Russia, Germany, and Japan. Unlike these countries, the U.S. population increases because of a growing number of immigrants.[19]

Annual percentage rates of population growth, 2010–2020, for China, Germany, Japan, Russia, and the United States are 0.4, -0.1, -0.4, -0.5, and 1.0, respectively, in comparison with the 1 percent annual growth rate of total world population for the same period.[20] It is reasonable to speculate that an economic cataclysm is on the way as population declines in some countries.

10.4 GEOECONOMIC IMPLICATIONS OF FOOD CONSUMPTION IN POOR COUNTRIES

History informs us that conflicts and wars have political, ideological, religious, and racial connections. From the perspective of economists, however, the ultimate goal of conflicts and wars rests on economic interests. We have witnessed political tensions and confrontations in connection with energy and natural resources. Food is not an exception. In addition to oil from the Caucasus region, Germany was interested in the Ukrainian granary during World War II. Germany wanted to resettle part of its population in forcibly depopulated agricultural lands of the USSR. During World War II, a considerable number of Japanese resettled in Korea and shipped rice they produced on farmlands obtained in Korea to their home country. The Japanese government required each Korean

Table 10.3. Insurance and Pensions by Country: 2010 (percent of GDP)

	Direct Gross Premiums	Health Expenditures	Practicing Physicians	Contributions to Pension Funds	Benefits paid by Pension Funds
U.S.	11.4	16.0	2.4	3.4	4.5
Australia	5.6	NA	3.0	8.9	4.9
Austria	5.6	10.5	4.6	0.4	0.2
Belgium	8.2	11.1	3.0	0.4	0.3
Canada	7.3	10.4	NA	3.2	2.7
Finland	3.9	8.4	2.7	9.8	10.5
France	10.4	11.2	NA	NA	NA
Germany	6.6	10.5	3.6	0.3	0.2
Italy	7.7	9.1	NA	0.6	0.2
Japan	8.3	NA	2.2	0.4	0.2
Korea, S.	11.1	6.5	1.9	0.2	0.3
Luxembourg	44.1	6.8	2.8	0.9	0.1
Mexico	1.7	5.9	2.0	0.6	0.2
Netherlands	7.9	9.9	NA	5.3	3.9
Norway	5.6	8.5	4.0	0.5	0.3
Spain	5.7	9.0	3.6	0.6	0.4
Sweden	5.8	9.4	NA	NA	NA
Switzerland	10.0	10.7	3.8	8.4	5.5
U.K.	14.5	8.7	2.6	2.7	3.2

Sources: U.S. Census Bureau, *Statistical Abstract of the United States*: 2012, p. 855. OECD, *OECD Insurance Statistics Database and Health Data*.

farm household to comply with their forced program, the so-called public collections of allotted amount of rice, in addition to confiscations of aluminum and copper wares. In August 2010, a Russian embargo of grains to Egypt caused a panicky situation of food shortage that led to political unrest in Egypt and eventually resulted in regime change.

There is a shortage of food in the world at present. The shortage can easily become a common problem across countries in parts of the world. For example, China (population of about 1.4 billion) and India (population of 1.2 billion) are now facing a shortage of food that might become a calamity in both countries and extend elsewhere in Asia.[21] One can imagine a worst-case scenario of severe shortages of food in the world. Massive starvation would prevail, followed by exclusion policies in Europe and the United States in response to the massive exodus of desperate people from Africa to southern Europe and from the Central America to the United States.

NOTES

1. Note that the budget effect that may be referred to as the "income effect" and aforementioned price effect are the effects in the different context from the Slutsky equation (the total effect) that consists of the Hicks-Allen net substitution effect and income effect. See Chung (1994) for theoretical and empirical references.

2. Reimer and Hertel (2004) reported empirical results that are consistent with Engel's law for certain items. Estimated values of the income elasticity of meat consumption in Tanzania and China (poor countries) are above unity, and those in Japan, the United States and Switzerland (rich countries) are below unity, respectively. According to Foroohar (*Time*, February 28, 2011, p. 19), people in poor countries spend higher percentages of their incomes on food as food prices rise, whereas rich countries spend lower percentages of their incomes on food.

3. Office of the Federal Register, National Archives and Records Administration, *The United States Government Manual 1993/1994*, Washington, DC: U.S. Government Printing Office, 1993, p. 133.

4. See endnote 6 of chapter 9.

5. The Common Agricultural Policy (CAP) is a system of target prices for farm products combined with import barriers and export subsidies in the EU, led by France. It was criticized by the United States and an interest group of nineteen agricultural exporting countries, often called Cairns Group, formed in 1986, including Australia, Canada, Argentina, Brazil, some of the South American countries, and some of the ASEAN. The United States sought a significant reduction of EU's subsidies for a greater access of U.S. farm goods in the EU. In December 1993, both countries agreed to compromise on the agreement on agricultural products.

6. See Chung (2006) for discussions in detail.

7. The FAO, *Statistical Yearbook*, 2012, p. 12 and p. 14.

8. The supply schedule is equivalent to the marginal cost (MC) schedule in case of perfect competition.

9. An increase in food prices was inflationary by 70 percent in developing countries, 13.9 percent in the U.S., 17.0 percent in Canada, and 22.7 percent in Japan in 2007, according to the IMF. Estimated rate of inflation as a result of higher expected price of crops in the EU was revised from 2.6 percent to 4.28 percent in 2008.

10. There are numerous biblical records on famine and poverty, some of which are stated in the history of the world. For historical records on poverty, see Roberts, J. M., *The New History of the World*, Oxford University Press, 2003.

11. See UNDP (United Nations Development Programme), *Human Development Report* 2014.

12. Malthus (1798).

13. Kunzig (2011) pp.42–63.

14. Ehrlich (1968) and Garreau (2006), 96–104.

15. Kunzig,(2011).

16. It means a combination of improved seeds, irrigation systems, pesticides, fertilizers for more grain production.

17. See Chung (2006).

18. The U.N. and the U.S. Bureau of the Census project that by 2025: one-fifth of the population of the world will be the population of China and that the significant number of one-fourth of the population of the world over sixty-five who live in poor areas in China need support.

19. Garreau, 2006.

20. U.S. Bureau of the Census, *Statistical Abstract of the United States*, 2012, pp. 837–38.

21. China is currently the most populous country but is already below replacement fertility presumably because of its required one-child policy. According to the UN's medium-term projection, population of India will rise over 1.6 billion people by 2050. By 2030, the population of India is expected to exceed the population of China.

Conclusion

Today's world is virtually under the control of superpowers. A dynamic force in the geoeconomic competition of superpowers stemming from global economic disparity (GED) motivates them to pursue their economic and political interests in international markets. Conflicts of interest in international markets among superpowers, often involving political and military interventions, result in a corresponding global historical event (GHE), either in the form of an agreement or a crisis/war. Logically, global stability requires the global economy to remain in an equilibrium situation. However, the equilibrium situation is constantly subject to external disturbances and a temporary equilibrium is not necessarily synchronized by national and international policies. Furthermore, a few superpowers, as *political* oligopolists, have no interest in turning the global economy competitive. In general, economists believe that free trade under competition ensures global equilibrium and achieves it by reducing trade barriers. The World Trade Organization (WTO) and policy makers in every member country have strived to maintain freer trade since the GATT of 1947. It is necessary for all countries to keep international markets competitive for free trade. However, free trade is not sufficient. No superpower depends only on trade policies that are narrowly scoped. Although mutually exclusive, a coordinated use of economic policies, international politics, and military strategies is what superpowers leave on the global stage. Overall, economic principles are necessary but not sufficient. This limitation signifies geoeconomic perspectives on such a colossal subject as the relationships between economic disparities prevailing among many geographical areas or countries in all industrial sectors and their consequences.

This book proposes a global policy toward a *larger* number of superpowers in order to promote competition in the global market that is consistent with the principle of inter-regional and inter-country competition. In other words, a multilevel competition is an efficient way to deal with GED-GHE causalities in the world. It diversifies global economic risks, including global financial crisis, and will facilitate the political stability in the world. This proposition is a radical departure from the conventional trade policy that focuses on lowering trade barriers. It is not intended to reject the standard trade policy but to suggest that such a policy is not sufficient for the case of a few superpowers.

Prior to World War I, superpowers existed only in Europe. After the war, the United States began to emerge as a superpower and has become the most powerful superpower in the world since World War II. In Asia, Japan was expanding for about two decades prior to World War I and also benefited from the loss of some European colonies in Asia after World War I. After World War II, Japan became the only superpower, followed now by rapid economic growth in other Asian countries such as South Korea, Singapore, and Taiwan. China, still underdeveloped and poor in terms of per capita income, has recently emerged as a superpower. At present, India has a high potential to become another emerging superpower. Asia as a whole has made a significant paradigm shift over the long-standing global economic hegemony of the West. The emergence of the Asian economy is meaningful, not just for Asia but for the entire world. As another superpower as a bloc, it surely makes significant contributions to the world market to be competitive along with the United States and Europe. Emergence of the Latin American economy along with Central America is desirable for the same reason. It is hoped that Argentina, Brazil, Chile, and Mexico will display their leadership for regional economic growth and political stability over the coming decades. There are differences in endowments of resources between the East Asian economy and Latin American economy. With heavy investment in education, East Asia has been successful in developing human resources, the prime engine for economic growth in Asian countries. With abundant natural resources, Latin America has a great potential for economic growth in the future with investment in education and technological development. Africa is underdeveloped presumably because of its history of severe colonial exploitation and inherent problems such as poverty and diseases. Multilevel competition among a larger number of superpowers would also alleviate the problems in the third world countries.

The central part in global economic disparities (GEDs) is international transactions—goods and services and capital flows. It is a collective representation of economy-wide structural imbalances among countries in all areas. Deficits repeatedly accumulated over time in a country, simply its mounting debt by definition (GED), result eventually in a financial crisis (GHE). In the recent past, there were numerous crises in Latin America and Asia. The latest crises are those in the United States and euro countries. It has been a period of turbulence in the global economy for almost a decade now, and its impact appears be continuing for a while in the future.This book reviews the financial crisis in the United States and its contagions at Europe as a major GED-GHE phenomenon. The Fed responded to the crisis by means of quantitative easing (QE), implemented in three successive phases. The QE policy has contributed to stabilize the U.S. economy in crisis. However, the U.S. economy has been undergoing a recession for several years. Labor and investment in the United States have remained historically low, yielding a surprising aggregate tolerance of economic slack. On the other hand, there have been fears among economists about hyper-inflation that may result from such a super-expansionary monetary policy. Contrary to the public fears, there has not been hyper-inflation so far, presumably because the excessively high rate of unemployment precipitated expectations drawn on the long-run Phillips curve trade-off phenomenon. The Fed had been deliberately scrutinizing the timeframe for ending the QE policy and finally ended it on November 29, 2014.

Technically, the balance of payments, either surplus or deficits, reflects the overall status of international transactions that may be examined in each subject area broken down into human resources incorporated with investment and technology, materials, energy, environment, and food and poverty. This book confirms strong correlations between economic disparities prevailing in all areas and corresponding historical events. GEDs are self-adjusting through multilevel competition. However, the world community should exert itself to minimize global economic disparities for global economic stability and political peace.

This book is a pioneering work in terms of the subject area and the approach to it. It confirms the GED-GHE causalities prevailing under the global system of a few superpowers. A larger number of competitive superpowers, that is, a multilevel competitive system of the global economy, optimizes the causalities and diversifies global risks.

Bibliography

CHAPTER 1

Acemoglu, Daron, and James Robinson, *Why Nations Fail: The Origins of Power, Prosperity, and Poverty*, New York: Crown Business, 2012.

Barraclough, Geoffrey, ed., *The Times Atlas of World History*, Sixth Concise Edition, London: Times Books, 1997.

Chung, Jae Wan, *The Political Economy of International Trade: U.S. Trade Law, Policy, and Social Cost*, Lanham, MD: Lexington Books, 2006.

Council of Economic Advisors, *Economic Report of the President*, Washington, D.C.: U.S. GPO, 2012.

Economist.com/special reports, "A Third Industrial Revolution," *The Economist*, April 21st–27th, 2012, pp. 3–20.

Greenspan, Alan, *The Age of Turbulence: Adventures in a New World*, New York: Penguin Press, 2007.

Krugman, Paul, "Increasing Returns, Monopolistic Competition, and International Trade," *Journal of International Economics*, Vol . 9, No. 4, November 1979, 469–79.

Roberts, J. M., *The New History of the World*, New York: Oxford University Press, 2002.

Stiglitz, Joseph E., *Globalization and Its Discontents*, New York: W.W. Norton and Company, 2002.

CHAPTER 2

Chung, Jae Wan , "International Market Shares and Global Economic Power," *Japan and the World Economy* 3 (1991), pp. 1–16.

———, *Political Economy of International Trade*, Lanham, MD: Lexington Books, 2006.

Council of Economic Advisors, *Economic Report of the President*, Washington, DC: U.S. Government Printing Office, 2011, pp. 89–93.

Deng, Yong and Fei-Ling Wang, eds., *China Rising: Power and Motivation in Chinese Foreign Policy*, Lanham, MD: Rowman & Littlefield, 2005.

Ferguson, Nial, *Civilization: The West and the Rest*, New York: Penguin Books, 2011.

Hayek, Friedrich A., *Law, Legislation and Liberty*, Vol. II, *The Mirage of Social Justice*, Chicago: University of Chicago Press, 1976.

Hook, Steven W. and John Spanier, *American Foreign Policy Since World War II*, 17th ed., Washington, DC: CQ Press, 2007.

Kissinger, Henry, *Diplomacy*, New York: Simon & Schuster, 1994.

Liu, Guoli, ed., *Chinese Foreign Policy in Transition*, New Brunswick, NJ: Aldine Transaction, 2007.

Melvin, Michael, *International Money and Finance*, 7th ed., Boston: Pearson Addison-Wesley, 2004.

Roberts, J. M., *New History of the World*, Oxford: Oxford University Press, 2002.

Snow, Donald M., *United States Foreign Policy*, 3rd ed., Belmont, CA: Wardsworth, 2005.

Twining, Daniel, "CSIS," *Washington Quarterly*, Summer 2007.

"X" (George F. Kennan), "The Sources of Soviet Conduct," *Foreign Affairs*, XXV (4), July 1947, pp. 566–82.

CHAPTER 3

Barro, Robert, "Are Government Bonds Net Worth?" *Journal of Political Economy*, 82 (6), pp. 1095–1117.

Chung, Jae Wan, "International Market Shares and Global Economic Power," *Japan and World Economy* 3, 1991, pp. 1–16.

———, *Political Economy of International Trade: U.S. Law, Policy, and Social Cost*, Lanham, MD: Lexington Books, 2006.

Dornbusch, Rudiger, *Open Economy Macroeconomics*, New York: Basic Books, 1980.

Krugman, Paul R. and Maurice Obstfeld, *International Economics: Theory and Policy*, 6th ed., Boston: Addison Wesley, 2003.

McArdle, Megan, "Europe's Real Crisis," *Atlantic*, April 2012, pp. 32–35.

CHAPTER 4

Bernanke, Ben S., "Nonmonetary Effects of the Financial Crisis in Propagation of the Great Depression," *American Economic Review* 73, no. 3, June 1983, 27–76

Congleton, Roger D. "On the Political Economy of the Financial Crisis and Bailout of 2008–2009," *Public Choice* 140, September 2009, pp. 287–317.

Council of Economic Advisors, *Economic Report of the President*, Washington, DC: U.S. Government Printing Office, 2005–2013.

Friedman, Milton and Anna Jacobson Schwartz, *A Monetary History of the United States, 1896–1960*, Princeton, NJ: Princeton University Press, 1963.

Giddy, Ian H., *Global Financial Markets*, Lexington, MA: D. C. Heath and Company, 1994, 297–317.

IMF, *World Economic Outlook*, Washington, DC: 2005–2013.

Krugman, Paul R. and Maurice Obstfeld, *International Economics, Theory and Policy*, Boston: Addison Wesley, 2007.

Melvin, Michael, *International Money & Finance*, Boston: Pearson Addison-Wesley, 2004, pp. 237–49.

OECD, *OECDStatEstracts*, Brussels, Belgium: 2013.

Ricards, James S., *Currency Wars: The Making of the Next Global Crisis*, Penguin Group, 2011.

Shiller, Robert J., *Irrational Exuberance*, Princeton, NJ: Princeton University Press, 2nd ed., 2000.

U.S. Department of Commerce, Bureau of the Census, *Statistical Abstract of the United States*, Washington, DC: U.S. Government Printing Office, 2006 and 2012.

CHAPTER 5

Chung, Jae Wan, *Political Economy of International Trade: U.S. Trade Laws, Policy, and Social Cost*, Lanham, MD: Lexington, 2007.

Davis, Gary W., "Eastern Way: How Chinese Philosophy Can Power Innovation in Business Today," *Innovation Management*, June 18, 2012, p. 2.

IMF, *World Economic Outlook*, Washington, DC: 2005–2013.

Krugman, Paul R. and Maurice Obstfeld, *International Economics, Theory and Policy*, Boston: Addison Wesley, 2007.

Melvin, Michael, *International Money and Finance*, Boston: Pearson Addison-Wesley, 2004.

Muellbauer, John, *Financial Times*, November 2008.

Sharma, Ruchir, *Breakout Nations: In Pursuit of the Next Economic Miracle*, New York: W. W. Norton, & Company, 2013.

Zakaria, Fareed, "China's Economy Running Low on Rocket Fuel," *Washington Post*, May 24, 2012, p. A21.

CHAPTER 6

Chung, Jae Wan, *The Political Economy of International Trade: U.S. Trade Law, Policy, and Social Cost*, Lanham: Lexington Books, 2006.

Clark, Don P., "Recent Evidence on Determinants of Intra-Industry Trade," *Weltwirtschaftliches Archiv*, 1993.

Davis, Gary W., "Eastern Way: How Chinese Philosophy Can Power Innovation in Business Today," *Innovation Management*, June 18, 2012, p. 2.

Grubel, Herbert G. and Peter J. Lloyd. *Intra-industry Trade*, London: Macmillan, 1975.

Schumpeter, Joseph A, "The Analysis of Economic Change," *Review of Economics and Statistics*, 1955.

———, "Economic Theory and Entrepreneural History," *Change and Entrepreneur*, 1949.

———, History of Economic Analysis, 1954 (published posthumously. Ed., Elisabeth Boody Schumpeter), 1954.

Solow, Robert M., "A Contribution to the Theory of Economic Growth," *Quarterly Journal of Economics*, February 1956, pp. 65–94.

CHAPTER 7

Barraclough, Geoffrey, ed., *The Times Atlas of World History*, 6th ed., London: Times Books, 1998, pp. 100–101.

Chung, Jae Wan, "The Effects of Material Costs on Inflation in U.S. Manufacturing Industries," *Applied Economics* 1, 1979, pp. 271–87.

———, *Utility and Production Functions: Theory and Applications*, Oxford: Blackwell, 1994.

Eckstein, O. and G. Fromm, "The Price Equation," *American Economic Review* 58, December 1968, pp. 1159–84.

Humphrey, David B. and J. R. Moroney, "Substitution among Capital, Labor and Natural Resource Products in American Manufacturing," *Journal of Political Economy* 83, February 1975, pp. 55–87.

Kunzig, Robert, "There Will Soon Be Seven Billion People on the Planet," *National Geographic*, January 2011, pp. 42–68.

Nordhaus, W. D., "Recent Development of Price Dynamics," in O. Eckstein (ed.), *The Econometrics of Price Determination*, Board of Governors of the Federal Reserve System and Social Science Research Council, 1972, pp. 16-49.

Oxford University Press, *Essential World Atlas*, 6th ed., London: Philip's, 2011, pp. 26–27.

Stigler, George S., *The Concentration of Industry*, Homewood, IL: Richard Irwin, 1968. UN Convention on the Law of the Sea.

———, "The Kinky Oligopoly Demand Curve and Rigid Prices," *Journal of Political Economy* 55, October 1947, 432–46.

CHAPTER 8

Berndt, Ernst R. and David Wood, "Technology, Prices, and the Derived Demand for Energy," *Review of Economics and Statistics*, Vol. 57, August 1975, pp. 259–268.

Chung, Jae Wan , "On the Estimation of Factor Substitution in the Translog Model," *Review of Economics and Statistics* 64, no. 1, 1987, pp. 409–17.

———, "The Price of Gasoline, the Oil Crisis, and the Choice of Transportation Mode," *Quarterly Review of Economics and Business* 21, no. 3, Autumn 1981, pp. 77–86.

Griffin, J. M. and P. R. Gregory, "An Intercountry Translog Model of Energy Substitution Responses," *American Economic Review* 66, December 1976, pp. 845–57.

Halvorsen, R., "Energy Substitution in U.S. Manufacturing," *Review of Economics and Statistics* 59, November 1977, pp. 381–88.

Houthakker, Hendrik S. and L. D. Taylor, *Consumer Demand in the United States 1929–1970*, 2nd ed., Cambridge, MA: Harvard University Press, 1970.

Hudson, E. A. and Dale W. Jorgenson, "U.S. Energy Policy and Economic Growth, 1975–2000, *Bell Journal of Economics and Management Science* 5, Autumn 1974, pp. 461–514.

Oxford University Press, *Oxford Essential World Atlas*, 6th ed., New York: 2011, p. 25.

Pindyck, Robert S., "Interfuel Substitution and the Industrial Demand for Energy: An International Comparison," *Review of Economics and Statistics* 61, May 1979, pp.169–79.

Supperville, Darlene and Dina Capiello, "U.S. Oil Production to Speed Up," AP, May 14, 2011.

CHAPTER 9

Barnosky, Anthony D. and 21 Scientists, "Approaching a State Shift in Earth's Biosphere," *Nature*, June 7, 2012.

Barraclough, Geoffrey, ed., *The Time Atlas of World History*, London: Time Books, pp. 4–5.

Becker, Gary S., "Crime and Punishment: An Economic Approach," *Journal of Political Economy* 76, no. 2, March 1968, pp. 169–217.

Becker, Gary S. and Casey B. Muligan, "Deadweight Costs and the Size of Government," *Journal of Law and Economics* 46, no. 2, October 2003, pp. 293–340.

Chung, Jae Wan, *Political Economy of International Trade: U.S. Trade Law, Policy, and Social Cost*, Lanham, MD: Lexington Books, 2006, pp. 194–200.

Coase, Ronald, "Nature of the Firm," *Economica* 4 no. 16, 1937, p. 386.

———, "The Problem of Social Cost," *Journal of Law and Economics* 3, no. 1, 1960, pp. 1–44.

Congleton, Roger, D., "Political Institutions and Pollution Control, *Review of Economics and Statistics* 74, no. 3, August 1992, pp. 412–21.

IMF, *World Economic Outlook*, October, 2007.

Joughlin, Ian, Benjamin E. Smith, and Brooke Medley, "Marine Ice Sheet Collapse Potentially Underway for the Thwaites Glacier Basin, West Antarctica," *Science*, May 16, 2014, pp. 735–38.

National Climate Assessment, *Our Changing Climate*, Washington, DC: U.S. Government Ppinting Office, May 6, 2014.

Oxford University Press, *Oxford Essential World Atlas*, 6th ed., New York: Oxford University Press, 2011, p. 4.

von Neuman, John and Oscar Morgenstern, *Theory of Games and Economic Behavior*, Princeton, NJ: Princeton University Press, 2004.

CHAPTER 10

Chung, Jae Wan, *The Political Economy of International Trade: U.S. Trade Law, Policy, and Social Cost*, Lanham, MD: Lexington Books, 2006.

———, *Utility and Production Functions: Theory and Applications*, Cambridge, MA: Blackwell Publishers, 1994.

Ehrlich, Paul R., *The Population Bomb*, New York: Ballantine Books, 1968.

Food and Agriculture Organization of the United Nations, *FAT Statistical Yearbook*, 2008 and 2013.

Garreau, Joel, "300 Million and Counting," *Smithsonian*, October 2006, pp. 96–104.

Houthakker, Hendrik S., "An International Comparison of Household Expenditure Patterns, Commemorating the Centenary of Engel's Law," *Econometrica* 25, October 1957, 532–51.

Joughlin, Ian, Benjamin E. Smith, and Brooke Medley, "Marine Ice Sheet Collapse Potentially Underway for the Thwaites Glacier Basin, West Antarctica," *Science*, May 16, 2014, pp. 735–38.

Kunzig, Robert, "There Will Soon Be Seven Billion People on the Planet." *National Geographic*, January 2011, pp. 42–68.

National Climate Assessment, *Our Changing Climate*, Washington, DC: U.S. Government Printing Office. May 6, 2014.

Reimer, Jeffrey and Thomas Hertel, "Estimation of International Behavior for Use with Input-Output Based Data," *Economic Systems Research* 16 no. 4, 2004, pp. 347–66.

Roberts, J. M., *New History of the World*, Oxford: Oxford University Press, 2002.

Index

About the Author

Jae Wan Chung is Professor *Emeritus* of Economics at George Mason University, Fairfax, Virginia. He received his Bachelor of Commerce degree from Seoul National University and PhD in economics from New York University in 1972 and subsequently began to teach both undergraduate and graduate courses at George Mason University the same year. Professor Chung served briefly at the World Bank as a consultant and at the Inter-American Defense College as a seminar consultant. He also served as a visiting professor of the Economics Division, Seoul National University, held positions at the Research Department, the Bank of Korea, and as dean of the College of Economics and Business Administration, University of Suwon, Korea. In addition, he served as a senior visiting research fellow, International Economic Institute, and research advisor to the International Economic Policy Institute in Korea during his sabbaticals from George Mason University. Professor Chung is the author of numerous articles published widely in scholarly journals. He is the author of books:

- *Utility and Production Functions: Theory and Applications*, Blackwell Publishers, 1994.
- *Political Economy of International Trade: U.S. Trade Law, Policy, and Social Cost*, Lexington Books, 2006.